JAPAN NOW!

A JAPANESE LANGUAGE READER

ERIKO SATO
ANNA SATO

TUTTLE Publishing
Tokyo | Rutland, Vermont | Singapore

"Books to Span the East and West"

Tuttle Publishing was founded in 1832 in the small New England town of Rutland, Vermont [USA]. Our core values remain as strong today as they were then—to publish best-in-class books which bring people together one page at a time. In 1948, we established a publishing outpost in Japan—and Tuttle is now a leader in publishing English-language books about the arts, languages and cultures of Asia. The world has become a much smaller place today and Asia's economic and cultural influence has grown. Yet the need for meaningful dialogue and information about this diverse region has never been greater. Over the past seven decades, Tuttle has published thousands of books on subjects ranging from martial arts and paper crafts to language learning and literature—and our talented authors, illustrators, designers and photographers have won many prestigious awards. We welcome you to explore the wealth of information available on Asia at **www.tuttlepublishing.com**.

Published by Tuttle Publishing, an imprint of Periplus Editions (HK) Ltd.

www.tuttlepublishing.com

Copyright © Eriko Sato and Anna Sato

All rights reserved. No part of this publication may be reproduced or utilized in any form or by any means, electronic or mechanical, including photocopying, recording, or by any information storage and retrieval system, without prior written permission from the publisher.

All photos from Shutterstock

Library of Congress Publication Data in process

ISBN 978-4-8053-1784-6

29 28 27 26 25
10 9 8 7 6 5 4 3 2 1   2502VP
Printed in Malaysia

TUTTLE PUBLISHING® is a registered trademark of Tuttle Publishing, a division of Periplus Editions (HK) Ltd.

Distributed by

North America, Latin America & Europe
Tuttle Publishing
364 Innovation Drive
North Clarendon
VT 05759-9436 U.S.A.
Tel: 1 (802) 773-8930
Fax: 1 (802) 773-6993
info@tuttlepublishing.com
www.tuttlepublishing.com

Japan
Tuttle Publishing
Yaekari Building 3rd Floor
5-4-12 Osaki Shinagawa-ku,
Tokyo 141 0032
Tel: (81) 3 5437-0171
Fax: (81) 3 5437-0755
sales@tuttle.co.jp
www.tuttle.co.jp

Asia Pacific
Berkeley Books Pte. Ltd.
3 Kallang Sector #04-01, Singapore 349278
Tel: (65) 6741-2178
Fax: (65) 6741-2179
inquiries@periplus.com.sg
www.tuttlepublishing.com

Contents

Preface 4
How to Use This Book 5

THE STORIES
Sexual Minority Rights 8
Cosplay: The Art of Dressing Up 16
Nature and the Environment 24
The Origins of Sake 34
Maiko, Apprentice Geisha 42
Omae: A Question of Language 52
Aging Japan 62
Is K-Pop Beating J-Pop in the Globalization of Asian Music? 72
Irezumi: Japan's Underground Tattoo Culture 82
Japanese Women Break the Iron Ceiling 92
Why Are the Japanese So Bad at English? 104
Japan's High Suicide Rate 116
Transforming Japan's Way of Working 130
Japan's Drinking Culture 140
Dating Opportunities 154
Why I Love Japan Even More since the Earthquake 164
Dealing with Godless Japan 184

Appendix I: Verb Forms 200
Appendix II: Adjective Forms 202
Answer Key 203
References 204

Preface

JAPAN NOW! A Japanese Language Reader gives you an insider glimpse into many aspects of real Japan as it is today, through seventeen essays focusing on stories about real people and real social issues and cultural trends. The topics include aging, romantic relationships, drinking culture, LGBTQ rights and much more. Each essay is laid out in parallel Japanese and English versions on facing pages. You'll see essays written by different authors, each with a distinctive style and point of view. Most importantly, each of the seventeen essays lets you see the human side of Japan, so you can hear people's voices and feelings as you learn about the latest facts, figures and trends.

You can enjoy reading the essays in English, but if you are studying Japanese, you can challenge yourself to read the Japanese versions of the essays. You'll find this easier if you already know the hiragana and katakana alphabets and at least fifty kanji characters, along with basic vocabulary and grammar. Don't be discouraged if the essays seem a little difficult at first—you can always quickly peek at the English text, provided in parallel on the facing page. You'll also find key Japanese grammar points explained and a comprehensive Japanese–English vocabulary list for every essay. There are comprehension questions too, and discussion questions, to help you expand and reinforce your Japanese skills as you immerse yourself in authentic Japanese and deepen your appreciation of each story.

We hope you enjoy these seventeen stories about contemporary Japan and that they will enrich both your knowledge of this fascinating country and your language skills.

How to Use This Book

This book has seventeen chapters along with appendices (conjugation tables), answer keys and a list of sources. Earlier essays are comparatively easier and shorter than later essays. Each story has the following components:

♦ **Introduction**
Three keywords and a relevant photo will prime you for each essay.

♦ **Japanese Text**
The Japanese text of each essay is written in natural and authentic Japanese language so you can experience "real" Japanese. Kanji characters are provided with *furigana* (a pronunciation guide written in small hiragana, above each kanji character) the first time it appears in a paragraph. If it is repeated in that paragraph, furigana are not given, to help you start to read fluently, without any props. Audio recording of Japanese texts (downloadable from Tuttle's website, see facing page) help you learn natural pronunciation, intonation, rhythm and speed in Japanese and improve your listening comprehension.

♦ **English Text**
English text is provided next to the Japanese text for each essay, to refer to if needed. Although the English and Japanese texts have equivalent meanings, the way the meaning is conveyed may differ because of the differences between the English and the Japanese languages. Don't be surprised when you notice the following differences:

1. The passive voice is used more in Japanese than in English.
2. Second and third person pronouns are rarely used in Japanese, unlike in English.
3. Singular and plural noun forms in Japanese are usually the same, unlike in English.
4. In Japanese, relationships between phrases and sentences are expected to be contextually understood in most cases. In English these relationships would need to be articulated with transition words, like *and*, *but* or *then*.

5. Sentences tend to be longer in Japanese than in English, and commas are used less frequently in Japanese than in English.

♦ Vocabulary and Expressions

Most content words and idiomatic expressions in the stories are listed in the "Vocabulary and Expressions" section of each chapter.

1. To make it easier for you to find words, the list is divided by paragraph numbers that correspond to the paragraph numbers indicated in the text.
2. Brief grammar information is provided with some words and phrases using terms such as "stem-form," "**te**-form," "plain form," and "passive form," which are listed in Appendices I and II. You can learn how they are used in context by looking at the Japanese text.
3. For each essay, a new word is only given once, in the first paragraph where it appears, so you need to read each essay from the beginning. However, words listed in earlier essays are listed again when they appear in subsequent essays, so you can start with any essay without missing key vocabulary words.

♦ Comprehension and Language

This section provides gapfill or multiple-choice questions to help you review the content of the essay, the grammar points and the vocabulary words. An answer key is provided on page 203. The questions are ordered following the order of content in the essay. So, if you finish all questions, you will be able to naturally review and summarize the essay. Question sentences in this section are written in plain styles (with verbs ending in だ **da** and た **ta**) while most essays are written in polite styles (with verbs ending in です **desu** and ました **mashita**). In this way, you can become accustomed to both plain and polite writing styles.

♦ Discussion Points

This section provides a few open-ended and thought-provoking questions. You can write down your responses in English or Japanese, or you can discuss them with your classmates or study-mates. These questions can help you deepen your appreciation of the issues covered in each essay and relate them to your own experiences.

◆ **Online Audio Files**

Audio recordings of each story are provided at the link below to help you learn natural intonation, rhythm and speed in Japanese and improve your listening comprehension.

How to access the audio recordings for this book:

1. Check to be sure you have an Internet connection.
2. Type the URL below into to your web browser.

    https://www.tuttlepublishing.com/japan-now

For support you can email us at info@tuttlepublishing.com.

Sexual Minority Rights

The Japanese courts have recently declared that a ban on same-sex marriage is unconstitutional. Is Japanese society finally becoming more inclusive?

Key words

性的マイノリティ **seiteki mainoritī** sexual minority

権利 **kenri** right

同性カップル **dōsei kappuru** same-sex couple

Part 1

In 2023, the BBC ran the story of Aki and Hikari, a lesbian couple with a baby, who found it difficult to rent a place to live together in Tokyo. They were told by a real estate agent that the property they were interested in was only for couples, despite the fact that they were a couple. This is just one of the many hardships that same-sex couples face in Japan.

性的マイノリティの権利
Seiteki mainoriti no kenri

Part 1

2023年、BBCは、赤ちゃんのいるレズビアン・カップル、アキさんとヒカリさんが東京でいっしょに住める賃貸物件を探していたときに経験した困難について報じました。借りたいと思った物件は不動産業者からカップル専用であるので不可だと言われました。アキさんとヒカリさんもカップルであるにもかかわらずです。これは同性カップルが直面する多くの困難の一つに過ぎません。

Part 2

According to historian Gary Leupp, homosexuality, particularly male-male relationships known as *nanshoku* (male colors), was not culturally taboo in Japan until the Meiji era (1868–1912), when the country was exposed to the Western world and Christianity, which criticizes homosexuality. However, as the BBC article points out, Japan is now the only G7 country that does not fully recognize same-sex couples or offer them clear legal protection.

Part 3

Nonetheless, Japan has made some progress since the Meiji era. In 2015, Shibuya Ward in Tokyo issued the first same-sex partnership certificate in Japan. In 2021, the Sapporo District Court ruled that the ban on same-sex marriage was unconstitutional, marking the first such decision in Japan. This was a significant step toward the legalization of same-sex marriage, although many more steps are still needed.

Part 4

Same-sex "partnerships" in Japan do not grant the full legal rights and benefits of marriage, such as inheritance rights and spousal visas. However, embracing diversity is increasingly important in global business, diplomacy and cultural exchanges. Aki and Hikari hope that the day will come when they are able to legally marry in Japan, and that the children of gay couples will grow up in a society that is free from discrimination.

Part 2

　歴史家のゲイリー・リュープ氏によれば、同性愛、特に「男色」として知られていた男性同士の同性愛は、日本ではもともと文化的にタブー視されてはいませんでした。しかし、明治時代（1868年－1912年）になって西洋の世界とキリスト教に接触したことで、同性愛が批判されるようになったそうです。ですが、BBCの記事が指摘するように日本は現在、主要7カ国（G7）の中では同性カップルを完全に認めていない、また同性カップルに明確な法的な保護を与えていない唯一の国です。

Part 3

　それでも、明治時代以降、多少の進展は日本でもありました。2015年、東京都渋谷区は日本ではじめて同性パートナーシップ証明書を発行しました。2021年には、札幌地方裁判所が日本ではじめて同性婚禁止は違憲であると判断しました。まだ道のりは長いですが、これは同性婚の合法化に向けた大きな一歩でした。

Part 4

　日本での同性の「パートナーシップ」には、結婚にともなう法的権利や利益、たとえば相続権や配偶者ビザなどが完全には認められていません。しかし、ダイバーシティー（多様性）を受け入れることは、グローバルなビジネス、外交、文化交流においてますます重要になってきています。アキさんとヒカリさんは、いつか日本で合法的に結婚できる日が来ることを願っています。そして、同性カップルの子供たちが、差別のない社会で育つことを望んでいます。

Vocabulary and Expressions

PART 1

- 年 **...nen** year ...(e.g., 1963, 2024)
- 赤ちゃん **akachan** baby
- 住める **sumeru** to be able to live (potential form of 住む **sumu** to live)
- 賃貸 **chintai** rental
- 物件 **bukken** property
- 探す **sagasu** to look for
- ...ときに **... toki ni** when ...ing (following a verb in the plain form)
- 同性 **dōsei** same-sex
- 経験する **keiken suru** to experience
- 困難 **konnan** difficulty
- ...について **... ni tsuite** about ...
- 報じる **hōjiru** to report
- 借りる **kariru** to rent
- ...たい **...tai** to want to do ... (following a verb in the stem form)
- ...と思う **... to omou** to think ...
- 不動産業者 **fudōsangyō-sha** real estate agent
- 専用 **senyō** exclusive
- 不可 **fuka** impossible
- 言われる **iwareru** to be told (passive form of 言う **iu** to tell)
- ...にもかかわらず **... ni mo kakawarazu** despite ...
- 直面する **chokumen suru** to face directly
- 多くの **ōku no** many
- ...の一つに過ぎない **... no hitotsu ni suginai** to be just one of ...

PART 2

- 歴史家 **rekishika** historian
- ...氏 **... shi** honorific suffix used after someone's name
- ...によれば **... ni yoreba** according to ...
- 同性愛 **dōseiai** homosexuality
- 特に **toku ni** especially
- 男色 **nanshoku** male-male homosexuality in the Edo era
- ...として **... toshite** as ...
- 知られている **shirarete iru** to be known
- 男性同士 **dansei dōshi** between men
- もともと **motomoto** originally
- 文化的に **bunkateki ni** culturally

タブー視される **tabū-shi sareru** to be viewed as taboo

明治時代 **Meiji jidai** the Meiji era

西洋 **seiyō** the West; Western countries

世界 **sekai** world

キリスト教 **Kirisuto-kyō** Christianity

接触する **sesshoku suru** to contact

批判する **hihan suru** to criticize

…ようになる **…yō ni naru** to start …ing (following a verb in the plain non-past form)

…そうだ **…sō da** they say that … (following a verb or an adjective in the plain form)

ですが **desuga** however

記事 **kiji** (newspaper) article

指摘する **shiteki suru** to point out

…ように **…yō ni** as … (following a verb in the plain form)

現在 **genzai** currently

主要7カ国 **Shuyō Nana-ka-Koku** G7

完全に **kanzen ni** completely

認める **mitomeru** to recognize; to approve

明確な **meikaku na** clear

法的な **hōteki na** legal

保護 **hogo** protection

与える **ataeru** to give

唯一の **yuiitsu** only

国 **kuni** country

PART 3

それでも **soredemo** however; nonetheless

…以降 **… ikō** since …; after …

多少の **tashō no** some; to some extent

進展 **shinten** progress

東京都 **Tōkyō-to** Tokyo Metropolis

渋谷区 **Shibuya-ku** Shibuya Ward

証明書 **shōmeisho** certificate

はじめて **hajimete** for the first time

発行する **hakkō suru** to issue

札幌 **Sapporo** Sapporo (a city in Hokkaido)

地方裁判所 **chihō saibansho** district court

同性婚 **dōsei-kon** same-sex marriage

禁止 **kinshi** ban; prohibition

違憲 **iken** unconstitutional

Seiteki mainoriti no kenri

判断する **handan suru** to judge

道のり **michinori** distance; path

長い **nagai** long

合法化 **gōhōka** legalization

…に向けた **... ni muketa** toward ...

一歩 **ippo** one step

PART 4

結婚 **kekkon** marriage

…にともなう **... ni tomonau** accompanying ...

権利 **kenri** rights

法的 **hōteki** legal

利益 **reiki** benefit

たとえば **tatoeba** for example

相続権 **sōzoku-ken** inheritance right

配偶者ビザ **haigū-sha biza** spousal visa

多様性 **tayosei** diversity

受け入れる **ukeireru** to receive; to accept

外交 **gaikō** diplomacy

文化交流 **bunka kōryū** cultural exchange

ますます **masumasu** increasingly

重要だ **jūyō da** to be important

(…て)くる **(...te) kuru** to have come to ... (following a verb in the **te**-form)

願う **negau** to hope; to pray

子供 **kodomo** child

…たち **...tachi** plural suffix for people and animals

差別 **sabetsu** discrimination

社会 **shakai** society

育つ **sodatsu** to grow up

望む **nozomu** to hope; to wish

Comprehension and Language

Select the most appropriate answer in the parentheses or fill in the gap.

1. アキさんとヒカリさんは、物件を（買い・借り）たいと思っていた。

2. アキさんとヒカリさんが好きだった物件は、不動産業者からカップル専用なので（不可・可能）だと言われた。

3. これは同性カップルが直面する多くの＿＿＿＿＿の一つに過ぎない。

4. 同性愛がタブー視されはじめたのは＿＿＿＿時代になってからだ。

5. 日本がキリスト教（に・で）接するようになってから、同性愛が批判されるようになった。

6. ２０１５年に東京都渋谷区ではじめて同性＿＿＿＿＿＿証明書を発行した。

7. ２０２１年に札幌地方裁判所がはじめて同性婚禁止は＿＿＿＿＿だと判断した。

8. 同性パートナーシップには＿＿＿＿＿権や、配偶者ビザが認められていない。

9. 多様性を＿＿＿＿＿ことは日本のグローバルなビジネスにも重要だ。

10. アキさんとヒカリさんは、同性カップルの子供たちが差別のない社会で育つ＿＿＿＿＿を望んでいる。

Discussion Points

1. Do you know any countries that support the rights of sexual minorities? Give some examples of how those countries support sexual minorities.
2. Do you know any countries that do not support the rights of sexual minorities? What could be the main reasons?

Cosplay: The Art of Dressing Up
by Héctor García

Author Héctor García describes Japan's cosplay culture, where people dress as characters from manga, anime and video games.

> **Key words**
>
> 集まる **atsumaru** to gather
>
> レイヤー **reiyā** cosplayer
>
> 趣味 **shumi** hobby, pastime

Part 1

The word cosplay comes from the Japanese word *kosupure*, which derives from the English words "costume" and "role-play." The cosplay subculture is made up of people who like dressing up as characters from manga, anime and video games, or as famous singers, superheroes or movie monsters. They usually form communities and meet to talk about how

コスプレ：
ドレッシングアップのアート
Kosupure: Doresshingu appu no āto
エクトル・ガルシア

Part 1

英語のcosplayという言葉は、日本語の「コスプレ」から来ていますが、これはカタカナ英語の「コスチューム」と「ロールプレイ」を組み合わせたものです。コスプレのサブカルチャーは、マンガ、アニメ、ビデオゲームのキャラクターや、有名な歌手、スーパーヒーロー、映画のモンスターなどに仮装して楽しむ人達で成り立っています。この人達はたいていコミュニティーを作り、集まってどのような改善が最新の衣装になされたのか、グループ

they've improved their latest costume, what accessories and improvements they need for the group, and where to buy things to complement their costumes. It's a whole world, a hobby with its own customs.

Part 2

For instance, cosplayers (those who practice cosplay) will organize photo shoots during which they place themselves against a wall, and *kameko* (amateur photographers who want to take pictures of them) form lines. The kameko wait, and when their turn comes, they have a few minutes to photograph the cosplayers in different poses they've rehearsed for the occasion. Very often the kameko will print some of their best photographs and give them to cosplayers as gifts.

Part 3

Cosplayers also organize competitions at conventions and at cosplay clubs in Tokyo's Akihabara district. At the clubs, a cosplayer ranking is created, with the best in each group competing against each other, and ultimately there are rankings at the national level, which are published in specialty magazines.

Part 4

Cosplayers gather at events like the Tokyo Game Show and Comiket (the world's largest amateur manga convention). They routinely gathered around Harajuku Station on Saturdays and Sundays at noon before it was redeveloped in the late 2010s. Now, cosplayers gather in Takeshita Street and Yoyogi Park instead.

に必要なアクセサリーや改善点は何か、コスチュームに合わせる小物や道具はどこで購入できるかなどについて話し合います。これは独自の文化をもつ趣味の世界と言えるでしょう。

Part 2

たとえば、コスプレイヤーまたはレイヤー（コスプレをする人）は、写真撮影会を企画し、壁に並んで立ち、カメコ（レイヤーを撮影したいアマチュアカメラマン）が列を作ります。カメコは順番を待ち、自分の番が来ると、レイヤーを数分間撮影しますが、その間レイヤーはこの機会のためにリハーサルした様々なポーズをしてあげます。カメコはよくベストショットを印刷してレイヤーにプレゼントしてあげます。

Part 3

レイヤーは、秋葉原のコンベンションやクラブでコンテストも開催します。クラブでは、グループ内で最も優れたレイヤー達が競い合い、最終的に全国レベルのランキングが作られ、専門雑誌に掲載されます。

Part 4

レイヤーは、東京ゲームショーやコミケ（世界最大級のアマチュアによるマンガ展示会）などのイベントで集まります。2010年代後半に再開発される前は、土曜日と日曜日の正午に原宿駅周辺に集まっていました。しかし、現在では竹下通りや代々木公園に集まるようになりました。

Part 5

Cosplay as a hobby has existed in Japan since the 1980s. It has gradually spread to elsewhere in Asia and is now becoming fully international. You will seldom see a manga or anime event or trade fair without a cosplay competition.

Vocabulary and Expressions

PART 1

英語 **eigo** English

…という **... to iu** called ...

言葉 **kotoba** word

コスプレ **kosupure** cosplaying

組み合わせる **kumi-awaseru** to put together

有名な **yūmei na** famous

歌手 **kashu** singer

映画 **eiga** movie

仮装する **kasō suru** to dress up in a costume as a disguise

楽しむ **tanoshimu** to enjoy oneself

人達 **hitotachi** people

成り立っている **naritatte iru** to be composed of

作る **tsukuru** to make; to form

集まる **atsumaru** to gather

改善 **kaizen** improvement

最新の **saishin no** the newest

衣装 **ishō** costume; attire

なされる **nasareru** to be done

必要な **hitsuyō na** necessary

点 **ten** point, aspect

…に合わせる **... ni awaseru** to fit with ...

小物 **komono** small thing

道具 **dōgu** tool

購入 **kōnyū** purchase

…など **... nado** etc.

…について **... ni tsuite** regarding ...; about ...

話し合う **hanashiau** to discuss

独自 **dokuji** unique

Part 5

　コスプレは、1980年代から日本で趣味として存在しており、少しずつアジアの他の地域に広がり、現在では完全に国際的なものとなりつつあります。マンガ／アニメのイベントや展示会でコスプレ・コンテストが開催されないことはほとんどありません。

文化 **bunka** culture

趣味 **shumi** hobby, pastime

世界 **sekai** world

言える **ieru** can be said (potential form of 言う **iu** to say)

PART 2

たとえば **tatoeba** for example

レイヤー **reiyā** cosplayer

写真 **shashin** photo

撮影 **satsuei** photo-taking

…会 **...kai** … meeting

企画する **kikaku suru** to organize

壁 **kabe** wall

並ぶ **narabu** to line up

立つ **tatsu** to stand

列を作る **retsu o tsukuru** to form a line

順番を待つ **junban o matsu** to wait one's turn

自分の番 **jibun no ban** one's own turn

数分間 **sūfunkan** for a few minutes

機会 **kikai** opportunity

…のために **... no tame ni** for … (following a noun)

様々な **samazama na** a variety of

印刷する **insatsu suru** to print out

PART 3

秋葉原 **Akihabara** Akihabara (Tokyo district)

開催する **kaisai** to host; to hold (events)

グループ内 **gurūpu-nai** within a group

最も **mottomo** most

優れる sugureru to excel

競い合う kisoi-au to compete against each other

最終的に saishūteki ni ultimately; eventually

全国レベル zenkoku reberu national level

作られる tsukurareru to be made (passive form of 作る tsukuru to make)

専門 senmon specialty

雑誌 zasshi magazine

掲載する keisai suru to post

PART 4

最大 saidai biggest

…級 ...kyū ... level

展示会 tenjikai exhibition, trade show

…年代 ... nendai decade (e.g., 1990年代 1990s)

後半 kōhan the latter half

再開発する sai-kaihatsu suru to redevelop

…前 ... mae before ...

土曜日 Doyōbi Saturday

日曜日 Nichiyōbi Sunday

正午 shōgo noon

原宿駅 Harajuku-eki Harajuku Station

…周辺 ... shūhen around ...

現在 genzai current; currently

竹下通り Takeshita-dōri Takeshita Street

代々木公園 Yoyogi-kōen Yoyogi Park

…ようになる ...yō ni naru to start ...ing (following a verb in the plain non-past form)

PART 5

存在する sonzai suru to exist

少しずつ sukoshi zutsu little by little

アジア Ajia Asia

他 hoka other

地域 chiiki region

広がる hirogaru to spread

完全に kanzen ni completely

国際的な kokusaiteki na international

…つつある ...tsutsu aru to be in the process of ... (following a verb in the stem form)

Cosplay: The Art of Dressing Up

Comprehension and Language

Select the most appropriate answer in the parentheses or fill in the gap.

1. 「コスプレ」はカタカナ英語の（コストューム・コスチューム）と、ロールプレイを組み合わせたものだ。
2. コスプレ・サブカルチャーで仮装して楽しむ人達は独自の文化をもつ＿＿＿＿の世界にいると言えるだろう。
3. コスプレをする人はコスプレイヤーまたは＿＿＿＿と言う。
4. レイヤーを撮影したいアマチュアカメラマンは＿＿＿＿と言う。
5. レイヤーは、秋葉原のクラブやコンテスト（に・で）コンペティションも開催する。
6. 最終的に全国レベルのランキングが（作・作られ）る。
7. 世界最大級のアマチュアによるマンガ展示会を（コミック・コミケ）と言う。
8. コスプレは少しずつアジアの他の地域に（広がった・広がらなかった）。

Discussion Points

1. What festivals do you know of around the world where young people get together? What activities take place at these festivals?
2. What do you think is the attraction of cosplaying?

Nature and the Environment

Is Japan effectively managing the recycling of all the waste it produces?

Key words

環境 **kankyō** environment

リサイクル **risaikuru** recycling

廃棄物 **haikibutsu** waste

Part 1

The old pond,
a frog jumps in,
the sound of water

Part 2

    This is one of the famous haiku by Basho, who profoundly loved nature. The love of nature is integral to Japanese culture and arts. Japanese gardens and bonsai recreate and miniaturize natural beauty, while tea ceremony and flower arranging emphasize harmony with the natural world. Hayao Miyazaki's anime films, such as *Princess Mononoke* and *Nausicaä of the Valley of the Wind*, also celebrate our deep connection with nature. This respect for nature is influenced by Buddhism and Shintoism.

自然と環境
Shizen to kankyō

Part 1

古池や
かわず飛びこむ
水の音

Part 2

　これは自然を深く愛した俳人、芭蕉の有名な俳句の一つです。自然への愛は日本の文化や芸術に欠かせないものです。日本庭園や盆栽は自然の美を再現し、縮小化しています。また、茶道と華道は自然との調和を強調しています。宮崎駿の『もののけ姫』や『風の谷のナウシカ』などのアニメもまた自然との深いつながりを称えています。この自然への敬意は、仏教や神道の影響を受けたものでしょう。

Part 3

The Japanese people's love for nature is also reflected in their efforts to protect the environment. In Japan, waste separation and recycling were firmly established as everyday practices decades before they gained any traction in the West. All recyclables must be sorted and neatly placed for collection. Milk cartons are thoroughly washed, dried and flattened. Food trays are sorted into Styrofoam and transparent trays. Cans are sorted into aluminum and steel. Supermarkets provide separate collection spaces for each type of recyclable. In some cities, household waste is divided into more than ten categories.

Part 4

Japan has also been a pioneer in reducing exhaust emissions. In 1997, Toyota launched the Prius, the world's first mass-produced hybrid car. Additionally, Japan is at the forefront of developing hydrogen-hybrid trains. Hydrogen is a clean energy carrier used to generate power, produce heat and provide fuel for transportation.

Part 5

However, there are limits to the capacity of recycling facilities within Japan, particularly for processing plastic waste. As a result, Japan sometimes sends plastic waste that cannot be processed domestically to other countries for processing, making the reduction of plastic waste a significant ethical challenge for the country. Additionally, nuclear power in Japan, while being a crucial part of the energy supply, has faced safety

Part 3

　日本人の自然への愛は環境保護への取り組みにも反映されています。日本では、廃棄物の分別とリサイクルが西洋で普及しはじめる何十年も前から日常的な習慣として確立されていました。すべてのリサイクル品は分類し、きちんと出さなければなりません。牛乳パックはきれいに洗って、乾かしてから平らにします。食品トレーは発泡スチロールと透明トレーに分けられます。缶はアルミとスチールに分けられます。スーパーには分別されたリサイクル可能な廃棄物の回収場所があります。一部の都市では、家庭ゴミが10種類以上に分けられることもあります。

Part 4

　また、日本は排出ガス削減の先駆者でもあります。1997年には、トヨタが世界初の量産型ハイブリッド車であるプリウスを発売しました。さらに、日本は水素ハイブリッド列車の開発の先駆者でもあります。水素は、電力を生成し、熱を生み出し、輸送用の燃料を供給するために使われるクリーンエネルギー源です。

Part 5

　しかし、日本国内のリサイクル施設には、プラスチックなどの廃棄物を処理する能力に限界があり、国内で処理できないプラスチック廃棄物を他の国に輸送し、処理してもらっていることもあります。そのため、プラスチック廃棄物を減らすことは日本にとって重要な倫理的課題となっています。また、2011年の東

and environmental challenges since the 2011 Tohoku earthquake and tsunami, which resulted in the meltdown of the Fukushima Daiichi Nuclear Power Plant.

Part 6

Japan, a country renowned for its ingenuity and innovation, must leverage its strengths further to address environmental challenges. This will be essential to overcome these obstacles, ensure a sustainable future and keep Japan's spiritual connection with nature alive.

Vocabulary and Expressions

PART 1

古池 **furuike** old pond

…や **... ya** a particle for a rhetorical pause with emotion (archaic)

かわず **kawazu** frog (archaic)

飛びこむ **tobikomu** to jump in

水 **mizu** water

音 **oto** sound

PART 2

自然 **shizen** nature

深く **fukaku** deeply

愛する **ai suru** to love

俳人 **haijin** haiku poet

芭蕉 **Basho** the name of one of Japan's most famous poets

有名な **yūmei na** famous

俳句 **haiku** haiku

愛 **ai** love

文化 **bunka** culture

芸術 **geijutsu** art

欠かせない **kakasenai** indispensable

庭園 **teien** landscaped garden

盆栽 **bonsai** bonsai (the art of growing miniature trees)

美 **bi** beauty

再現する **saigen suru** to recreate

28　*Nature and the Environment*

日本大震災による福島第一原発のメルトダウン以来、原子力は日本のエネルギー供給源の重要な部分でありながら、安全性や環境への影響に課題を抱えています。

Part 6

日本は、独創力と革新力の強さで知られる国です。環境問題に取り組むためにはこれらの強みをさらに活用し、障害を克服し、持続可能（サステイナブル）な未来を確保し、日本の自然への精神的なつながりを守り続けることが不可欠となるでしょう。

縮小化する **shukushō-ka suru** to miniaturize; to reduce in size

茶道 **sadō** the way of tea; Japanese tea ceremony

華道 **kadō** Japanese flower arranging

調和 **chōwa** harmony

強調する **kyōchō suru** to emphasize

宮崎駿 **Miyazaki Hayao** the name of one of Japan's most famous animators

姫 **hime** princess

風 **kaze** wind

谷 **tani** valley

深い **fukai** deep

つながり **tsunagari** bond; relationship

称える **tataeru** to commend; to honor; to praise

敬意 **keii** respect; esteem

仏教 **Bukkyō** Buddhism

神道 **Shintō** Shintoism

影響 **eikyō** influence

受ける **ukeru** to receive

PART 3

環境 **kankyō** environment

保護 **hogo** protection

取り組み torikumi undertaking

反映する hanei suru to mirror; to reflect

廃棄物 haikibutsu waste

分別 bunbetsu sorting; separation

西洋 seiyō the West

普及する fukyū suru to become widespread

…はじめる …hajimeru to start … (following a verb in the stem form)

何十年も前から nanjū-nen mo mae kara for many decades

日常的な nichijōteki na ordinary, routine

習慣 shūkan custom; habit

…として … toshite as …

確立する kakuritsu suru to (firmly) establish

…品 …hin item for …

分類する bunrui suru to classify

きちんと kichinto neatly

出す dasu to put out

…なければならない …nakereba naranai must …

牛乳パック gyūnyū pakku milk carton

きれいに kirei ni cleanly; neatly

洗う arau to wash

乾かす kawakasu to dry

平ら taira flat

食品トレー shokuhin torē food tray

発泡スチロール happō-suchirōru Styrofoam

透明トレー tōmei torē transparent tray

分ける wakeru to divide; to separate

缶 kan can

アルミ arumi aluminum

スチール suchīru steel

スーパー sūpā supermarket

可能な kanō na possible

回収 kaishū collection; retrieval

場所 basho place

一部 ichibu a portion

都市 toshi city; urban area

家庭 katei household

ゴミ gomi garbage

10種類 jusshurui ten categories

…以上 … ijō more than …

PART 4

排出ガス(はいしゅつ) **haishutsu gasu** exhaust gas; emissions

削減(さくげん) **sakugen** reduction; cutback

先駆者(せんくしゃ) **senku-sha** pioneer; forerunner

…年(ねん) **...nen** year ...(e.g., 1963, 2024)

世界初(せかいはつ) **sekai hatsu** world's first

量産型(りょうさんがた) **ryōsan-gata** mass-production type; mass-produced

ハイブリッド車(しゃ) **haiburiddo-sha** hybrid vehicle; hybrid car

発売(はつばい) **hatsubai** launch or release (of merchandise)

水素(すいそ) **suiso** hydrogen

ハイブリッド列車(れっしゃ) **haiburiddo ressha** hybrid train

開発(かいはつ) **kaihatsu** development; innovation

電力(でんりょく) **denryoku** electric power; electricity

生成する(せいせい) **seisei suru** to generate; to produce

熱(ねつ) **netsu** heat

生み出す(うみだす) **umidasu** to create; to generate

輸送(ゆそう) **yusō** transportation

…用(よう) **...yō** for ... (following a noun)

燃料(ねんりょう) **nenryō** fuel

供給する(きょうきゅう) **kyōkyū suru** to supply; to provide

…ために **...tame ni** for the purpose of ... (following a verb in the plain non-past form)

使われる(つか) **tsukawareru** to be used (passive form of 使う(つか) **tsukau** to use)

クリーンエネルギー **kurīn enerugī** clean energy

…源(げん) **...gen** source of ...

PART 5

国内(こくない) **kokunai** domestic; within the country

施設(しせつ) **shisetsu** facility

処理する(しょり) **shori suru** to process; to handle

能力(のうりょく) **nōryoku** ability; capability

限界(げんかい) **genkai** limitation

輸出する(ゆしゅつ) **yushutsu suru** to export

減らす(へ) **herasu** to reduce

重要な(じゅうよう) **jūyō na** important

倫理的な(りんりてき) **rinriteki na** ethical

課題(かだい) **kadai** issue; task

東日本大震災 **Higashi Nihon Daishinsai** Great East Japan Earthquake

福島第一原発 **Fukushima Daiichi Genpatsu** Fukushima Daiichi Nuclear Power Plant

…以来 **... irai** since ...; following ...

部分 **bubun** part; portion

…ながら **...nagara** while ... (following a verb in the stem form)

安全性 **anzensei** safety

環境 **kankyō** environment

影響 **eikyō** impact; influence

抱える **kakaeru** to hold; to carry; to have

PART 6

独創力 **dokusōryoku** ability to create original item or concept

革新力 **kakushinryoku** ability to innovate

強さ **tsuyosa** strength

知られている **shirarete iru** to be known

国 **kuni** country; nation

問題 **mondai** problem; issue

取り組む **torikumu** to tackle; to address

強み **tsuyomi** strength; advantage

さらに **sara ni** further; additionally

活用する **katsuyō suru** to utilize; to make use of

障害 **shōgai** obstacle; barrier; disability

克服する **kokufuku suru** to overcome; to conquer

持続可能な **jizoku kanō na** sustainable

未来 **mirai** future

確保する **kakuho suru** to secure; to ensure

精神的な **seishinteki na** spiritual

守る **mamoru** to protect

…続ける **...tsuzukeru** to continue ...ing (following a verb in the stem form)

不可欠 **fukaketsu** indispensable; essential

…となる **...to naru** to become ...

…でしょう **...deshō** I guess ...

Comprehension and Language

Select the most appropriate answer in the parentheses or fill in the gap.

1. 自然への愛は日本の文化や芸術（を・に）欠かせない。
2. 日本では廃棄物の分別と＿＿＿＿＿＿＿を何十年も前からしている。
3. 牛乳パックはきれいに洗って（乾かした・乾かして）から平らにする。
4. 日本は排出ガス（削減・普及）の先駆者でもある。
5. （プラスチック・牛乳パック）廃棄物を減らすことは日本にとって重要な倫理的課題だ。
6. 原子力は日本のエネルギー供給源の重要な部分で（ある・あり）ながら、安全性や環境への影響に課題を抱えている。
7. 日本では独創力と革新力を使って障害を（克服・再現）することが不可欠だろう。

Discussion Points

1. Are there any customs in your culture that show or imply an appreciation for nature? If so, give some examples.
2. What are the recycling expectations where you live? Are there community rules or systems that support environmental sustainability? Are the societal expectations in your town too high, or should they be higher? Provide examples.
3. Can you think of other examples that showcase Japan's strength in ingenuity and innovation?

The Origins of Sake

by Nancy Matsumoto and Michael Tremblay

Sake experts Nancy Matsumoto and Michael Tremblay look at the history of the Japanese drink that has gained huge popularity worldwide.

> **Key words**
> 酒 **sake** sake (Japanese rice wine)
> 神 **kami** god
> 米 **kome** rice

Part 1

Sake is so intertwined with the history of Japan that it appears in its foundational myths, first as an offering to divine spirits, who were presumed to delight in the drink. Mentions of sake can be found in the earliest histories of Japan, *The Kojiki* (Record of Ancient Things) and *The Nihonshoki* (Chronicles of Japan), which date back, respectively, to the seventh and eighth centuries. In one such story, the god of Omiwa Shrine in Nara is revealed to the legendary first-century-BC Emperor Sujin in a dream. He advises his mortal subject that an offering of sake will quell the plague then sweeping across Japan. The sake has the desired effect, and Omiwa—Japan's oldest standing shrine—has ever since been thought to enshrine the god of sake and of master brewers.

酒の起源
Sake no kigen
松本ナンシー／マイケル・トレンブレ

Part 1

酒は日本の歴史と深く結びついていて、古代から神々への供え物として大変喜ばれた飲み物として日本の創世神話に登場します。7世紀から8世紀にまとめられた日本で最も古い歴史書、『古事記』や『日本書紀』にも酒に関する記述があります。その中の一つの物語では、奈良の大神神社の神が、伝説の紀元1世紀の天皇、崇神天皇の夢に現れ、当時日本で広がっていた疫病を治めるために酒を捧げるよう勧めます。その後、酒がその効果を出しました。それで、大神神社―日本で最も古い神社―は酒と酒造りの神を祀る神社として知られるようになりました。

Part 2

Today the close associations between sake and Shintoism live on, and sake plays a role in purification rites, rituals, festivals and other auspicious occasions. In the Heian period (794–1185), sake brewing was carried out by Buddhist monks, who, over time, gave up these duties to commercial sake makers. Enjoying sake became a pastime not just for the aristocracy but for the ordinary citizen as well.

Part 3

The tradition of *naorai*, a ritual in which participants commune with the gods through the shared drink of sake, is perhaps the Shintoist feature that most closely resembles the Christian ritual of Eucharist, or Holy Communion. But unlike wine, sake's purity and divinity extends to the ingredients with which it is made. In every sake brewery, you will find a miniature shrine (*kamidana*) affixed to a wall, bearing offerings of sake. This is where sake makers pray for safety and success in brewing. And in every brewer, you will find a reverence for sake's ingredients—rice, water, yeast and koji mold—that is imbued with Shinto and Buddhist overtones.

Part 2

　今日でも、酒と神道は深く結びついており、酒は清めの儀式、お祭り、お祝いの場で大切な役目をしています。平安時代（794年－1185年）には、酒の醸造は仏教の僧侶によって行われていましたが、やがてその役割は商売としての酒造りをする人に引き継がれ、酒を楽しむことは貴族だけでなく、一般の人達の間でも広まりました。

Part 3

　なおらいという儀式では、酒を通じて神々と一体になると信じられています。この儀式はキリスト教の聖餐式に最も近いものと言えるでしょう。しかし、ワインとは違って、酒の純粋さと神聖さは、その原材料にまで及んでいます。どの酒蔵の壁にも神棚があり、そこには酒が供えられています。そこで酒造りの安全と成功を祈ります。また、酒造りに携わる人々は、酒の原材料の米、水、酵母、麹に敬意を持っていて、神道や仏教の精神が込められています。

Vocabulary and Expressions

PART 1

酒 **sake** sake (Japanese rice wine)

歴史 **rekishi** history

深く **fukaku** deeply

結びつく **musubitsuku** connected

古代 **kodai** ancient

神々 **kamigami** gods

供え物 **sonaemono** offering

…として **... toshite** as ...

大変 **taihen** greatly

喜ばれる **yorokobareru** to be appreciated (passive form of 喜ぶ **yorokobu** to be delighted)

飲み物 **nomimono** beverage; drink

創世神話 **sōsei-shinwa** creation myths

登場する **tōjō suru** to appear

世紀 **seiki** century

まとめられる **matomerareru** compiled

最も **mottomo** most

古い **furui** old

歴史書 **rekishisho** historical records

古事記 **Kojiki** The Kojiki (Record of Ancient Things)

日本書紀 **Nihon Shoki** The Nihon Shoki (Chronicles of Japan)

…に関する **... ni kansuru** related to ...

記述 **kijutsu** description

物語 **monogatari** story

奈良 **Nara** Nara (a city in Japan)

大神神社 **Ōmiwa-jinja** Ōmiwa Shrine

神 **kami** god

伝説 **densetsu** legend

紀元 **kigen** era

天皇 **tennō** emperor

崇神天皇 **Sujin Tennō** Emperor Sujin

夢 **yume** dream

現れる **arawareru** to appear

当時 **tōji** at that time

広がる **hirogaru** to spread (physically)

疫病 **ekibyō** epidemic

治める **osameru** to quell

…ために **...tame ni** for the purpose of ... (following a verb in the plain non-past form)

捧げる **sasageru** to offer; to give

38   *The Origins of Sake*

…よう勧める …yō susumeru to recommend … (doing something)

その後 sono go after that

効果 kōka effect

出す dasu to produce

酒造り sakezukuri sake brewing

祀る matsuru to enshrine

知られる shirareru to be known (passive form of 知る shiru to know)

…ようになる …yō ni naru to become …

PART 2

今日 konnichi these days

清め kiyome purification

儀式 gishiki ceremony

お祭り omatsuri festival

お祝い oiwai celebration

場 ba place

大切な taisetsu na important

役目 yakume role; duty

平安時代 Heian jidai Heian period (794–1185)

…年 …nen … year

醸造 jōzō brewing

仏教 Bukkyō Buddhism

僧侶 sōryo monk

…によって … ni yotte by …

行われる okonawareru to be carried out (passive of 行う okonau to carry out)

やがて yagate eventually

役割 yakuwari role

商売 shōbai trade; business

引き継がれる hikitsugareru to be inherited (passive of 引き継ぐ hikitsugu to inherit)

楽しむ tanoshimu to enjoy

貴族 kizoku aristocracy

…だけでなく … dake de naku not only …

一般の ippan no ordinary

人達 hitotachi people

…の間 … no aida among …; between …

広まる hiromaru to spread (conceptually, becoming popular or widely known)

PART 3

なおらい naorai a ritual meal (often after a ceremony or festival)

…を通じて … o tsūjite through …

一体 ittai one body

キリスト教 **Kirisutokyō** Christianity

聖餐式 **seisanshiki** Eucharist; Holy Communion

近い **chikai** close; near

…と言える **... to ieru** can be said ...

違う **chigau** different

純粋さ **junsuisa** purity

神聖さ **shinseisa** sacredness; holiness

原材料 **genzairyō** raw materials; ingredients

…まで及ぶ **... made oyobu** extends to ...

どの…も **dono ... mo** every ...

酒蔵 **sakagura** sake brewery

壁 **kabe** wall

神棚 **kamidana** household Shinto altar

供える **sonaeru** to offer; to dedicate

酒造り **sake-zukuri** sake brewing

安全 **anzen** safety

成功 **seikō** success

祈る **inoru** to pray

携わる **tazusawaru** to be involved in

原材料 **genzairyō** ingredients

米 **kome** rice

水 **mizu** water

酵母 **kōbo** yeast

麹 **kōji** koji (mold used in fermentation)

敬意 **keii** respect

持っている **motte iru** to have; to hold

精神 **seishin** spirit; mind

込められる **komerareru** to be infused; to be put into

Comprehension and Language

Select the most appropriate answer in the parentheses or fill in the gap.

1. 酒は日本の創世（会話・神話）に登場する。
2. 大神神社は日本で最も（古い・深い）神社だ。
3. 大神神社は酒と酒造りの神を祀る神社として知られる（こと・よう）になった。
4. 平安時代は_____年から1185年までだ。
5. 平安時代には酒の醸造は仏教の僧侶によって（行って・行われて）いた。
6. なおらいという儀式では、酒を通じて神々と一体になる（を・と）信じられている。
7. どの酒蔵の壁（にも・もに）神棚がある。
8. 酒の原材料は米と、_____と、酵母と、麹だ。

Discussion Points

1. Alcohol is often used in rituals around the world. Why do you think that is?
2. What is unique about sake and sake brewing in Japan, compared to how various alcohols are produced in other countries? What might it suggest about Japanese culture?

Maiko, Apprentice Geisha

A glimpse into the mysterious world of the maiko trainee geisha.

> **Key words**
> 芸者 **geisha** geisha
> 舞妓 **maiko** *maiko*, apprentice geisha
> 伝統 **dentō** tradition

Part 1

Geisha are traditional female performing artists who entertain guests through refined skills in singing, dancing, music and conversation especially in settings such as banquets or gatherings where male guests are present. Their intricate hairstyles and elaborate kimonos captivate tourists from overseas. One could say that geisha epitomize Japanese traditional elegance. However, the lesser known *maiko*, or apprentice geisha, are equally integral to the world of traditional performing arts that has spanned more than 350 years in Japan.

舞妓、見習い芸者
Maiko, minarai geisha

Part 1

芸者は日本の伝統的な女性芸能者で、主に男性客が集まる宴会や会合で、歌や踊り、楽器演奏、会話術などのすぐれた芸で客をもてなします。芸者の手の込んだ髪型や華やかな着物は外国からの観光客を魅了しています。芸者は日本の伝統的な優美さの象徴と言えるでしょう。しかし、あまり知られていない芸者の見習いである舞妓も、日本で350年以上続く伝統的な技芸の世界において同じく重要な存在です。

Part 2

Maiko live in an *okiya* geisha house, where they thoroughly study the traditional arts of the geisha for several years. They don't receive a salary, but instead, their housing, food and training costs are covered by the okiya. This arrangement allows maiko to focus on mastering their craft without financial strain.

Part 3

Until several decades ago, most of the girls who came to okiya were from poor families who sought loans from the okiya, to be repaid gradually through their daughters' work. Nowadays, such practices no longer exist. The young girls who come to okiya hail from various regions of Japan. They have completed compulsory education and are following their dreams of becoming maiko. However, the rules are strict. For example, Koen, an eighteen-year-old maiko, says that she is not allowed to carry a cellphone, date or have more than two days off a month.

Part 4

Lesley Downer, the author of *Geisha: The Secret History of a Vanishing World*, lived in Japan for many years and studied the culture of geisha and maiko. She emphasizes that, contrary to common misconceptions, geisha are not prostitutes but masters of traditional Japanese performing arts and the art of conversation, soothing the worries of wealthy and influential men who seek their companionship and attention. Downer

Part 2

　舞妓は置屋という芸者を住まわせる家に住み、数年間、伝統的な芸者の芸を徹底的に学びます。舞妓は給料はもらえませんが、住居、食事、訓練費用はすべて置屋に賄ってもらいます。それで舞妓はお金の心配をしないで、技芸の訓練に専念することができます。

Part 3

　数十年前までは、置屋に来る少女の多くがお金に困っている家庭の出身で、親が置屋からお金を借りて、そのお金は娘が働いて少しずつ返していくというのが一般的でした。しかし、今ではそのような慣習はなくなり、日本各地の若い女性たちが義務教育を終えてから舞妓になる夢を追いかけ置屋に来るようになりました。置屋では厳しい規則があります。例えば、18歳の舞妓のこえんさんは携帯電話を持つことやデートすることが許されていません。また、休みは月に二日だけだそうです。

Part 4

　『Geisha: The Secret History of a Vanishing World』の著者であるレスリー・ダウナーさんは長年日本に住み、芸者や舞妓の文化を研究しました。ダウナーさんは、芸者は娼婦だとよく誤解されているが、そうではなく、芸者は日本の伝統芸能と会話術の達人であり、富裕層の有力な男性たちにとって彼女たちはおもてなしと気配りで心を癒してくれる存在であることを強調してい

Maiko, minarai geisha

thinks that if geisha were to disappear, it could lead to the decline of the kimono industry and traditional Japanese arts.

Part 5

However, fewer women today are willing to work as geisha due to the archaic and strict rules that maiko must follow. This is a serious concern for Suzuno, who has been working as a geisha for over thirty-five years. "I do not want it [the geisha world] to disappear," she said. "I love Japan. I want people to value Japan as much as they do their own country."

Vocabulary and Expressions

PART 1

芸者 **geisha** geisha

伝統 **dentō** tradition

…的な **...teki na** suffix used to turn a noun into an adjective

女性 **josei** female

芸能者 **geinō-sha** performer

主に **omoni** mainly

男性 **dansei** man; male

客 **kyaku** guest

集まる **atsumaru** to gather

宴会 **enkai** banquet

会合 **kaigō** meeting or gathering

歌 **uta** song

踊り **odori** dance

楽器 **gakki** musical instrument

演奏 **ensō** performance

会話術 **kaiwajutsu** conversation skills

…など **... nado** things like …

すぐれる **sugureru** to excel or be excellent

芸 **gei** skills; art; performance

もてなす **motenasu** to entertain

ます。ダウナーさんは、もし芸者がいなくなってしまうと、着物産業や日本の伝統芸能が衰える可能性があると考えています。

Part 5

しかし、こえんさんが言っていたような舞妓が経験する古風な厳しい規則のため、今日では芸者希望者は減っています。35年以上芸者として活動しているすずのさんにとってこれは大きな悩みです。すずのさんは次のように言いました。

「なくなってほしくないから。日本が大好きだから。日本っていう自分の国を、自分のおうちと同じように考えてね、大切にしてほしいなって思いますね。」

手の込んだ **te no konda** elaborate
髪型 **kamigata** hairstyle
華やかな **hanayaka na** glamorous
着物 **kimono** kimono
外国 **gaikoku** foreign country
観光客 **kankōkyaku** tourist
魅了する **miryō suru** to fascinate; to captivate
優美さ **yūbisa** elegance
象徴 **shōchō** symbol
言える **ieru** to be able to say
  (potential form of 言う **iu** to say)
…でしょう **... deshō** I guess …
知られる **shirareru** to be known
  (passive form of 知る **shiru** to get to know)
見習い **minarai** apprentice
舞妓 **maiko** maiko apprentice geisha
…年 **...nen** … years
…以上 **... ijō** … or more
続く **tsuzuku** to continue
技芸 **gigei** performing arts
世界 **sekai** world

…において **... ni oite** in ...; within ...

同じく **onajiku** equally

重要な **jūyō na** important

存在 **sonzai** existence

PART 2

置屋 **okiya** okiya geisha house

…という **... to iu** called ...

住まわせる **sumawaseru** to let someone live

家 **ie** house

住む **sumu** to live

数年間 **sūnenkan** for several years

徹底的に **tetteiteki ni** thoroughly

学ぶ **manabu** to learn

給料 **kyūryō** salary

もらえる **moraeru** to be able to receive (potential form of もらう **morau** to receive)

住居 **jūkyo** housing

食事 **shokuji** meal

訓練 **kunren** training

費用 **hiyō** expense

賄う **makanau** to cover (the cost)

(…て) もらう **(...te) morau** to have someone do ... (following a verb in the **te**-form)

お金 **okane** money

心配 **shinpai** worry

技芸 **gigei** performing arts

専念する **sennen suru** to devote oneself

…ことができる **... koto ga dekiru** to be able to do ... (following a verb in the dictionary form)

PART 3

数十年前まで **sūjūnen mae made** until several decades ago

少女 **shōjo** girl

多く **ōku** many

困る **komaru** to struggle; to be in trouble

家庭 **katei** household; family

出身 **shusshin** one's birthplace

親 **oya** parent

借りる **kariru** to borrow

娘 **musume** daughter

働く **hataraku** to work

少しずつ **sukoshi zutsu** little by little

返す **kaesu** to return (something); to repay

(…て) いく **(...te) iku** to go on doing ... (following a verb in the **te**-form)

一般的 ippanteki typical, common

今 ima now

慣習 kanshū custom; regular practice

なくなる nakunaru to disappear; to be gone

各地 kakuchi various places

若い wakai young

義務教育 gimukyōiku compulsory education

終える oeru to finish; to complete

夢 yume dream

追いかける oikakeru to pursue

…ようになる …yō ni naru to start …ing (following a verb in the plain non-past form)

厳しい kibishii strict

規則 kisoku rule; regulation

例えば tatoeba for example

…歳 … sai … years old

その一人 sono hitori one of them

携帯電話 keitai denwa mobile phone

持つ motsu to have; to hold

許される yurusareru to be permitted (passive form of 許す yurusu to permit)

休み yasumi day off; break

月 tsuki month; the moon

二日 futsuka two days; the second of the month

…だけ … dake only …

…そうだ …sōda they say that … (following a verb or an adjective in the plain form)

PART 4

著者 chosha author

長年 naganen many years

文化 bunka culture

研究する kenkyū suru to research

娼婦 shōfu prostitute

誤解する gokai suru to misunderstand

達人 tatsujin expert; master

富裕層 fuyūsō wealthy class

有力な yūryoku na influential; powerful

…たち …tachi plural suffix for people and animals

…にとって … ni totte for …; in terms of …

彼女 kanojo she

気配り kikubari attentiveness; consideration

心を癒す kokoro o iyasu to soothe; to heal the heart

存在 sonzai existence

強調する kyōchō suru to emphasize

…しまう ...shimau to end up ...ing (with sense of regret) (following a verb in the **te**-form)

…と ...to if ... ; when ... (following a verb or an adjective in the plain non-past form)

産業 sangyō industry

衰える otoroeru to decline; to deteriorate

可能性 kanōsei possibility

考える kangaeru to think

PART 5

…ような ...yō na like ...; similar to ... (following a verb in the plain form)

経験する keiken suru to experience

古風な kofū na old-fashioned

厳しい kibishii strict

規則 kisoku rules; regulations

…のため ... no tame for the sake of ...

今日 konnichi nowadays

希望 kibō hope; desire

…者 ...sha (suffix) person associated with a particular role

減る heru to decrease

…として ... toshite as ...; in the role of ...

活動する katsudō suru to work; to be active

…にとって ... ni totte for. ..; in terms of ...

悩み nayami worry; trouble

次のように tsugi no yō ni as follows

…ほしい ... hoshii to want someone to ... (following a verb in the **te**-form)

…から ...kara because ... (following a verb in the plain form)

大好きだ dai suki da to love; to like very much

自分 jibun oneself

国 kuni country

おうち o-uchi home (polite form of うち uchi home)

同じ onaji same

考え kangae thought; idea

大切にする taisetsu ni suru to cherish; to value

思う omou to think

Comprehension and Language

Select the most appropriate answer in the parentheses or fill in the gap.

1. 芸者は日本の伝統的な優美さの象徴と(言える・言う)だろう。
2. 芸者の＿＿＿＿＿＿である舞妓も伝統的な技芸の世界で同じく重要な存在だ。
3. 芸者や舞子が住む家を＿＿＿＿＿＿と言う。
4. 給料はもらえないが、舞妓はお金の心配をしないで技芸の訓練に専念する（よう・こと）ができる。
5. もし芸者が（いなくなる・いなくなって）しまうと、着物産業や日本の伝統芸能が衰えるかもしれない。
6. しかし、置屋での古風な厳しい＿＿＿＿＿＿のため、芸者希望者は減っている。

Discussion Points

1. Why are geisha mistakenly associated with prostitution?
2. What can we do to eliminate such misconceptions?
3. Do you think the roles of geisha and maiko will change in the following few decades? Why or why not?

Maiko, minarai geisha

Omae: A Question of Language

In 2018, a superintendent of education resigned because he had offended his former student by addressing him with the informal term "omae."

> **Key words**
> 師弟関係 **shitei-kankei** teacher-student relationship
> 言葉遣い **kotoba-zukai** way of using language
> 立場 **tachiba** position or role (context dependent)

Part 1

Although the second-person pronoun is usually avoided when addressing or referring to a conversation partner in Japanese, there are several options for saying "you," such as *anata*, *kimi* and *omae*, all of which vary in formality and implication. An inappropriate choice can lead to serious issues in interpersonal relationships. In 2018, shocking news emerged from Japan due to such word choice.

おまえ：言葉遣いの問題
Omae: Kotoba-zukai no mondai

Part 1

日本語の会話では、相手を呼んだり相手について話したりするときに代名詞はたいてい避けますが、「あなた」、「君」、「お前」などを選ぶことはあります。これらの言葉は相手に対する敬意の度合いやニュアンスが違い、適切でないものを選ぶと、対人関係で大きな問題が起きることがあります。2018年、このような代名詞の選び方が原因で起きた衝撃的なニュースが日本で報じられました。

Part 2

The superintendent of education in a city in Niigata visited the family of a thirteen-year-old junior high school student who had committed suicide. The purpose of his visit was to formally apologize to the student's parents, as their son's suicide was due to bullying by his peers at the school.

Part 3

During their conversation, the superintendent asked the boy's father if he would like to join the upcoming PTA meeting to discuss the matter further. While the question was appropriate, the way it was phrased was questionable. He said, "Omae-mo kuru ka?" which roughly translates to "You coming?"

Part 4

The word *omae* is frequently used by men to address their subordinates, such as their students and assistants. It is not polite, but carries a tone implying closeness and familiarity. It so happened that the superintendent had been the father's homeroom teacher decades ago, and in Japan it is not unusual for the language of a former teacher-student relationship to be continued for a lifetime.

Part 5

However, being addressed as *omae* along with usage of the verb in an informal and casual style in such an emotionally sensitive context made the father feel disrespected and that the superintendent was taking his son's death lightly. The father must have complained about the misuse of the language by the superintendent. Within a week of this interaction, the superintendent resigned from his position, taking responsibility for his inappropriate language use. He said, with utmost formality: "The thought that I was his homeroom teacher in elementary school crossed

Part 2

新潟のある市の教育長が、その市の中学校で自殺した13歳の中学生の少年の家族を訪れました。目的は、少年の自殺は学校での同級生からのいじめが原因だったので、息子を失った両親にそのことについて正式に謝罪するためでした。

Part 3

教育長は会話の中で父親に今度のPTA会議に参加するかどうかを尋ねました。その質問自体は適切でしたが、その言い方に問題がありました。教育長は、「お前も来るか？」と言ったのです。

Part 4

「お前」は、男性が自分の生徒や部下などの目下の人に対して使うことが多く、丁寧ではありませんが、親しみが込められている響きがあります。実は、教育長は何十年も前にこの父親の担任教師をしていたことがありました。日本では、かつての師弟関係の言葉遣いが一生続くことは珍しくありません。

Part 5

しかし、この感情的に極限の状況で、非公式なくだけた言い方で「お前」と呼ばれたことで、父親は教育長に息子の死を軽く見られたと感じました。おそらく父親は教育長の言葉遣いについて申し立てをしたのでしょう。このやり取りの後、教育長は一週間以内に、自分の不適切な言葉遣いの責任を取って辞任しました。教育長は丁重に次のように述べました。

my mind [...]. I want to take responsibility for deeply hurting the feelings of the mourning family and significantly damaging trust in the Board of Education."

Part 6

One of the online comments on this issue emphasized the importance of putting oneself in another person's shoes.

"His first priority shouldn't be his own social standing, it should be concern for the victims. This is why he never noticed the bullying."

Vocabulary and Expressions

PART 1

会話 **kaiwa** conversation

相手 **aite** partner; other person

呼ぶ **yobu** to call; to address

(…た)り **(...ta)ri** to do ... and so on (following a verb in the ta-form)

…について **... ni tsuite** about ...; regarding ...

話す **hanasu** to talk; to speak

…ときに **... toki ni** when ...ing

代名詞 **daimeishi** pronoun

たいてい **taitei** usually

避ける **sakeru** to avoid

あなた **anata** you (formal or neutral)

君 **kimi** you (casual, often used among equals or to one's subordinate)

お前 **omae** you (informal, often used by men, can be seen as rude)

…など **...nado** etc.; and so on

選ぶ **erabu** to choose; select

言葉 **kotoba** words; language

…に対する **... ni taisuru** toward ...

敬意 **keii** respect; courtesy

「お父様の小学校時代の担任であったことが頭をよぎり、ふさわしくない発言にいたった。（中略）ご遺族の気持ちを深く傷つけ、教育委員会への信頼を著しく損ねる結果を招いた責任を取りたい。」

Part 6
　この問題についてのオンラインコメントの一つには、相手の立場に立つことの重要性が強調されていました。
「自分の立場に立つのではなく、被害者の気持ちを重んじて立ち位置を変えてほしい。だから、いじめに気がつかない。」

度合い **doai** degree; level
違う **chigau** to differ
適切な **tekisetsu na** appropriate; suitable

…と **...to** if ...; when ... (following a verb or an adjective in the plain non-past form)
対人関係 **taijin kankei** interpersonal relationships
問題 **mondai** issue; problem
起きる **okiru** to occur; to happen
…ことがある **... koto ga aru** there are times when ... (following a verb in the plain non-past form)
…年 **...nen** year ...(e.g., 1963, 2024)

原因 **gen'in** cause; reason
衝撃的な **shōgekiteki na** shocking
報じられる **hōjirareru** to be reported (passive form of 報じる **hōjiru** to report; to announce)

PART 2

新潟 **Nīgata** Niigata (a prefecture in northern Japan)
ある… **aru ...** a certain ...
市 **shi** city
中学校 **chūgakkō** junior high school
教育長 **kyōiku-chō** superintendent of education

自殺する jisatsu suru to commit suicide

…歳 ... sai ... years old

少年 shōnen boy

家族 kazoku family

訪れる otozureru to visit

目的 mokuteki purpose

学校 gakkō school

同級生 dōkyūsei classmate

いじめ ijime bullying

…ので ... node because ...

息子 musuko son

失う ushinau to lose

両親 ryōshin parents

正式に seishiki ni formally; officially

謝罪する shazai suru to apologize

…ため ...tame in order to ...

PART 3

父親 chichi-oya father

今度の… kondo no ... upcoming ...; next ...

会議 kaigi meeting; conference

参加する sanka suru to participate; to attend

…かどうか ...ka dō ka whether or not ...

尋ねる tazuneru to inquire

質問 shitsumon question

…自体 ... jitai ... itself

…が ...ga but ...

言い方 iikata way of speaking

問題 mondai problem; issue

言う iu to say

…のです ...no desu that's why ... (used to add an explanation)

PART 4

男性 dansei man; male

自分 jibun oneself

生徒 seito pupil

部下 buka subordinate

目下の人 meshita no hito subordinate; someone of lower status

…に対して ... ni taishite toward ...

使う tsukau to use

多い ōi numerous

丁寧 teinei polite; courteous

親しみ shitashimi closeness; familiarity

込められる **komerareru** to be filled with; to be imbued with (passive form of 込める **komeru** to put into)

響き **hibiki** tone; resonance

実は **jitsu wa** actually; in fact

何十年も前に **nanjūnen mo mae ni** decades ago

担任教師 **tannin kyōshi** homeroom teacher

…ことがある **... koto ga aru** to have an experience of ...ing (following a verb in the plain past form)

かつての **katsute no** former

師弟関係 **shitei-kankei** teacher-student relationship

基づく **motozuku** to be based on

言葉遣い **kotoba-zukai** language use

一生 **isshō** lifetime

続く **tsuzuku** continues

珍しい **mezurashii** rare; uncommon

PART 5

感情的な **kanjōteki na** emotional

極限 **kyokugen** extremity

状況 **jōkyō** circumstances; state of affairs

非公式な **hikōshiki na** informal; unofficial

くだけた **kudaketa** informal, friendly

死 **shi** death

軽い **karui** light; minor

感じる **kanjiru** to feel

おそらく **osoraku** probably; perhaps

申し立てをする **mōshitate o suru** to make a claim

…でしょう **...deshō** I guess ...

やり取り **yaritori** (communicative) exchange

…の後 **...no ato** after ...

一週間 **isshūkan** one week

…以内に **...inai ni** within ...

不適切な **futekisetsu na** inappropriate; unsuitable

責任を取る **sekinin o toru** to take responsibility

辞任 **jinin** resignation

丁重に **teichō ni** politely; with great care

次のように **tsugi no yō ni** as follows

述べる **noberu** to state

お父様 **o-tōsama** father (respectful form)

Omae: Kotoba-zukai no mondai 59

小学校 shōgakkō elementary school

…時代 ...jidai ... period; ...era

頭をよぎる atama o yogiru to flash through one's mind

ふさわしい fusawashii appropriate; suitable

発言 hatsugen utterance; remark

…にいたる ... ni itaru to lead to ...; to result in ...

中略 chūryaku omitted

ご遺族 go-izoku bereaved family (respectful form)

気持ち kimochi feelings; emotions

深く fukaku deeply

傷つける kizutsukeru to hurt, to wound

教育委員会 kyōiku iinkai board of education

信頼 shinrai trust, confidence

著しく ichijirushiku significantly, remarkably

損ねる sokoneru to damage; to harm

結果 kekka result; outcome

招く maneku to lead to; to bring about

PART 6

…の一つ ... no hitotsu one of ...

立場 tachiba position

立つ tatsu to stand

重要性 jūyōsei importance

強調する kyōchō suru to emphasize

被害者 higai-sha victim

重んじる omonjiru to value; to respect

立ち位置 tachiichi standing position, stance

変える kaeru to change

…ほしい ... hoshii to want someone to ... (following a verb in the te-form)

だから dakara therefore; so

…に気がつく ... ni ki ga tsuku to notice ...

Comprehension and Language

Select the most appropriate answer in the parentheses or fill in the gap.

1. 日本語の会話ではたいてい相手を呼ぶときに「あなた」を（避け・避けられ）る。
2. 不適切な二人称代名詞を（選んだ・選ぶ）と、対人関係で問題が起きるかもしれない。
3. 新潟のある中学校で少年が同級生の＿＿＿＿が原因で自殺した。
4. 教育長が正式に謝罪（する・し）ために少年の家族のうちに行った。
5. 会話の中で教育長は少年の父親を＿＿＿＿と呼んだ。
6. 教育長はかつて少年の父親の担任教師（だった・だ）からだ。
7. 少年の父親は教育長に息子の死を軽く見られた＿＿＿＿感じた。
8. 教育長は自分の不適切な言葉遣いの＿＿＿＿を取って辞任した。
9. オンラインコメントの一つは相手の＿＿＿＿に立つことの重要性を強調した。

Discussion Points

1. Have you ever changed the way you address someone? If so, why?
2. How does word choice impact human relationships in your culture? Are there words that are easily misinterpreted or misused? Give some examples.

Aging Japan

Japan is admired for its high number of centenarians, such as the celebrated Kin and Gin twins. But how is the quality of life for elderly citizens?

> **Key words**
> 高齢者 **kōrei-sha** elderly person
> 出生率 **shusshō-ritsu** birth rate
> 移民労働者 **imin rōdō-sha** immigrant workers

Part 1

At the start of the twenty-first century, Japan mourned the death of the famous twin sisters, Kin-san (Kin Narita) and Gin-san (Gin Kanie), who were born in 1892, and passed away at the ages of 107 and 108 respectively. To commemorate their 100th birthday, Kin and Gin recorded a rap song, which topped the Japanese pop charts. They once said, "We have been able to live long lives because we are twins." It was great that they were able to support and encourage each other.

高齢化する日本
Kōreika suru nihon

Part 1

21世紀のはじめに日本では有名な双子の姉妹の死を悼みました。きんさん（成田きん）と、ぎんさん（蟹江ぎん）です。二人は1892年生まれで、それぞれ107歳と108歳まで生きました。きんさんとぎんさんは、100歳の誕生日を記念してラップ曲でデビューし、日本のポップチャートで一位を獲得しました。きんさん、ぎんさんは「わしらは双子だったから長生きできたんだね」と言ったことがありました。お互いに支え合い、励まし合えたのがよかったのでしょう。

Part 2

While Kin and Gin touched the nation's hearts, longevity is not unusual in Japan. In 2021, the United Nations reported that Japan had the world's oldest population: three in ten people were aged 65 or over compared to one in ten worldwide. This is a testament to the country's healthy lifestyle practices and its robust healthcare system. On August 19, 2024, Maria Branyas Morera of Spain, aged 117, passed away, making Tomiko Itooka, aged 116, the world's oldest living person.

Part 3

On the other hand, Japan's birth rate recently hit a historic low. In 2023, fewer than 760,000 babies were born, the lowest number in 120 years and a 5 percent decrease from the previous year.

Part 4

The aging demographic in Japan can be tangibly felt by the increasing number of *akiya* vacant houses once lived in by elderly people. Many of these houses have cracked windows, vine-covered walls and crumbling rooftops, raising somber questions about whether the elderly residents lived lonely lives or died alone.

Part 5

Looking at these demographic changes, it is clear that Japan does not have enough young people to support and protect the nation. In 2019, a new residency status called "Specified Skilled Worker" was introduced, allowing a wider range of foreigners to work in Japan. However,

Part 2

　きんさんとぎんさんは、国民の心を打ちましたが、日本では長寿は珍しいことではありません。2021年、国連は日本が世界で最も高齢化が進んだ国であると報告しました。日本では、三人に一人が65歳以上です。世界全体の十人に一人に比べて非常に高い割合です。これは、日本の健康的なライフスタイルと充実した医療制度の賜物です。2024年8月19日にスペインのマリア・ブラニャス・モレラさん（117歳）が亡くなった後、世界最高齢者は日本の糸岡富子さん（116歳）になりました。

Part 3

　一方で、日本の出生率は近年、非常に低くなっています。2023年には、出生数が76万人以下になり、過去120年間で最低記録となりました。前年と比べると5%の減少です。

Part 4

　高齢者が亡くなり、残していった空き家が増えているのを見ると、日本の高齢化を実感せずにはいられません。これらの空き家には、ひび割れた窓、蔦に覆われた壁、そして崩れかけた屋根があることもあり、高齢者がそこで孤独な生活を送っていたのか、あるいは孤独死したのかという深刻な疑問を投げかけます。

Part 5

　このような人口の変化を見ると、日本には国を支えて守る若者が十分にいないことが分かります。2019年には、「特定技能」という新しい在留資格が導入され、より多くの外国人が日本

in addition to political and regulatory changes, Japanese society must also change. In an article by Professor Chris Burgess of Tsuda University on the website East Asia Forum, he says:

Part 6

"Migrants are often treated as guest workers, and their needs are not adequately addressed. The government should invest in proper infrastructure to address the disconnect between economic inclusion and social-political exclusion. As the need for labour increases, Japan needs to phase out its deeply entrenched ideology of a homogenous national identity to build a diverse and accepting society."

Vocabulary and Expressions

PART 1

世紀 seiki century

はじめ hajime beginning

有名な yūmei na famous

双子 futago twins

姉妹 shimai sisters

死 shi death

悼む itamu to mourn

二人 futari two people

…年生まれ …nen umare born in … (year)

それぞれ sorezore each

…歳 …sai … years old

…まで … made until …

生きる ikiru to live

誕生日 tanjōbi birthday

記念する kinen suru to commemorate

で働けるようになりました。しかし、それにともない、日本の社会も変わらなければなりません。津田塾大学のクリス・バージェス教授は、東アジアフォーラムのウェブサイトに掲載された記事で次のように述べています。

Part 6

「移民はしばしばゲストワーカーとして扱われ、彼らが必要な支援は十分に行われていません。政府は、経済的な理由では移民労働者を受け入れながらも社会的・政治的には排除しているというギャップを解消するために、適切なインフラに投資するべきです。労働力の需要が増える中で、昔からある日本は一つの民族で成り立っているという考え方を少しずつ捨て、多様性を尊重し、しっかりとした受け入れ体制を持つ社会を築く必要があります。」

ラップ曲 **rappu kyoku** rap song

一位 **ichi-i** first place

獲得する **kakutoku suru** to achieve

わしら **washira** we; us (dialect, slightly archaic)

…から **...kara** because …; since …

長生きする **nagaiki suru** to live long

言う **iu** to say

(…た) ことがあった **(...ta) koto ga atta** to have done … before (following a verb in the **ta**-form)

お互いに **otagai ni** each other

支える **sasaeru** to support

…合う **...au** to do … to each other

励ます **hagemasu** to encourage

PART 2

国民 **kokumin** citizen; people

心を打つ kokoro o utsu to touch the heart

長寿 chōju longevity

珍しい mezurashii rare

国連 Kokuren United Nations

世界 sekai world

最も mottomo most

高齢化 kōreika aging population

進む susumu to advance

国 kuni country

報告する hōkoku suru to report

…以上 … ijō more than …

全体 zentai whole

…に比べて … ni kurabete compared to …

非常に hijō ni extremely

高い takai high

割合 wariai proportion

健康 kenkō health

…的な …teki na suffix used to turn a noun into an adjective

充実した jūjitsu shita fulfilling

医療制度 iryō seido medical system

賜物 tamamono gift

亡くなる nakunaru to pass away

(…た)後 (…ta) ato after …ing (following a verb in the ta-form)

最… sai… most … (followed by a Sino-Japanese word)

高齢者 kōrei-sha elderly person

PART 3

一方で ippō de on the other hand

出生 shusshō birth (or 出生 shussei)

…率 …ritsu rate of …

近年 kinen recent years

低い hikui low

…数 …sū number of …

76万人 nanajūroku-man-nin 760,000 people

…以下 …ika fewer than …

過去120年間で kako 120-nenkan de in the past 120 years

最低記録 saitei kiroku record low

前年 zennen previous year

比べる kuraberu to compare

減少 genshō decrease

PART 4

残す nokosu to leave behind

68 Aging Japan

空き家 akiya vacant house

増える fueru to increase

…と ...to when ...ing; if ...ing (following a verb in the dictionary form)

高齢化 kōreika aging population

実感する jikkan suru to feel or realize

…せずにはいられない ...sezu ni wa irarenai cannot help but ...

多く ōku many (of them)

ひび hibi crack

割れる wareru to break

窓 mado window

蔦 tsuta ivy; vine

覆われる ōwareru to be covered (passive form of 覆う ōu to cover)

壁 kabe wall

崩れる kuzureru to collapse

…かける ...kakeru on the verge of ...

屋根 yane roof

孤独な kodoku na lonely

生活を送る seikatsu o okuru to lead a life; to live a life

あるいは aruiwa alternatively

孤独死 kodokushi dying along

深刻な shinkoku na serious

疑問 gimon question

投げかける nage-kakeru to raise

PART 5

人口 jinkō population

変化 henka change

支える sasaeru to support

守る mamoru to protect

若者 wakamono young person

十分に jūbun ni sufficiently

分かる wakaru to understand

特定技能 tokutei ginō specified skills

…という ... to iu called ...

新しい atarashii new

在留資格 zairyū shikaku residence status

導入される dōnyū sareru to be introduced (passive form of 導入する dōnyū suru to introduce)

より… yori ... more ...

多くの ōku no many

外国人 gaikokujin foreigner

働く hataraku to work

…ようになる **...yō ni naru** to start ...ing (following a verb in the plain non-past form)

それにともない **sore ni tomonai** along with that

社会 **shakai** society

変わる **kawaru** to change

…なければならない **...nakereba naranai** must ...

津田塾大学 **Tsuda Juku Daigaku** Tsuda University

教授 **kyōju** professor

東 **higashi** east

掲載される **keisai sareru** to be published (passive form of 掲載する **keisai suru** to publish)

記事 **kiji** article

次のように **tsugi no yō ni** as follows

述べる **noberu** to state

PART 6

移民 **imin** immigrant

しばしば **shibashiba** frequently

…として **...toshite** as ...

扱われる **atsukawareru** to be treated (passive form of 扱う **atsukau** to treat)

彼ら **karera** they

必要 **hitsuyō** necessary

支援 **shien** support

十分に **jūbun ni** sufficiently

行われる **okonawareru** to be carried out (passive form of 行う **okonau** to carry out)

政府 **seifu** government

経済 **keizai** economy

理由 **riyū** reason

労働者 **rōdō-sha** worker

受け入れる **ukeireru** to accept

…ながらも **...nagara mo** although ...

政治 **seiji** politics

排除する **haijo suru** to exclude

解消する **kaishō suru** to eliminate

…ために **...tame ni** in order to ...

適切な **tekisetsu na** appropriate

インフラ **infura** infrastructure

投資する **tōshi suru** to invest

Aging Japan

Comprehension and Language

Select the most appropriate answer in the parentheses or fill in the gap.

1. きんさんとぎんさんは双子の姉妹で、それぞれ107歳と108歳（から・まで）生きた。
2. 二人はお互いに支え（すぎた・合った）。
3. 2021年に国連は日本が世界で最も高齢（化・率）が進んだ国だと報告した。
4. しかし、近年の日本の出生（化・率）は非常に低い。
5. そのため、日本では（空き家・貸家）が増えている。
6. 日本には国を支えて守る若者が十分にいないから、移民＿＿＿＿＿者が必要だ。
7. 日本は彼らを受け入れるために適切なインフラに投資する（はず・べき）だ。
8. 日本は政治的にも社会的にも多様性を尊重（しないでは・しなければ）ならない。

Discussion Points

1. What is the general lifestyle like in your culture? Which practices are healthy and promote longevity? Which practices are not?
2. What is the healthcare system like in your culture? Which aspects are effective? Which are not?
3. What do you think are the factors contributing to the recent decline in Japan's birth rate?
4. Does your country accept or celebrate diversity? How do you know?

Is K-Pop Beating J-Pop in the Globalization of Asian Music?

K-Pop was developed following the Japanese model of the 1990s but diverged from J-Pop in the 2000s. How has K-Pop beaten J-Pop on the world stage?

Key words

歌 song

ダンス dance

歌詞 lyrics

Part 1

K-Pop has experienced explosive growth in the West over the past two decades, dominating pop-music charts and streaming platforms worldwide. However, the first Asian popular music artist to reach No. 1 in the US was a Japanese artist, Kyu Sakamoto. His song "Sukiyaki," topped the American Billboard Hot 100 in 1963. His blend of elements of traditional

アジア音楽のグローバル化では K-POP は J-POP に勝ったのだろうか

Ajia ongaku no gurōbaruka de wa K-Pop wa J-Pop ni katta no darō ka

Part 1

K-POP はこの 20 年間、西洋で爆発的な成長を遂げ、世界中のチャートやストリーミング・プラットフォームで上位を占めています。しかし、アメリカのビルボードではじめて一位を獲得したアジアのポップミュージック・アーティストは、日本の坂本九でした。彼の曲「上を向いて歩こう (Sukiyaki)」は 1963 年にアメリカのビルボード・ホット 100 で一位を獲得しました。坂本

Japanese music and American popular music laid the stepping stones for the formation of J-Pop.

Part 2

In Tokyo during the early 1960s, the talent agency Johnny & Associates began training and developing boy bands that could sing and dance in unison. They also significantly contributed to the formation of J-Pop, with bands including Four Leaves, who debuted in 1967, and SMAP, who debuted in 1991. According to journalist Naomi Gingold, SMAP and Johnny & Associates are largely responsible for laying out the blueprint for the K-Pop model.

Part 3

Professor Jayson Chun of the University of Hawaii says that K-Pop was developed on the Japanese model of the 1990s but diverged from J-Pop in the 2000s. Several factors contribute to this, but the most significant is K-Pop's ability to elevate the visual appeal of their groups, take dance to an entirely new level, and their proactive use of social media platforms such as TikTok and YouTube. The dance prowess of Korean artists enabled K-Pop to ride the wave of viral dance videos on TikTok and YouTube, which quickly attracted a young global audience. K-Pop idols' collaborations with international artists, along with their use of English and Japanese in their lyrics, have also contributed to K-Pop's global popularity, which has surpassed that of J-Pop.

九の邦楽の要素とアメリカのポピュラー音楽の要素を融合させたスタイルは、J-POPの形成において重要な礎を築きました。

Part 2

また1960年代のはじめ、東京でジャニーズ事務所という芸能プロダクションが誕生し、歌って踊れる男性アイドルグループの育成を開始し、J-POPの形成に大変役立ちました。例えば、1967年にデビューしたフォーリーブスや、1991年にデビューしたSMAPです。ジャーナリストのナオミ・ギンゴルドさんは、SMAPとジャニーズ事務所はK-POPモデルの青写真を築いたと述べています。

Part 3

ハワイ大学のジェイソン・チュン教授は、K-POPは1990年代の日本モデルを基に発展したが、2000年代にJ-POPから違う方向に進んだと述べています。その要因はいくつかありますが、最も重要なのは、K-POPのグループがビジュアル的な魅力を高め、ダンスをまったく新しいレベルに引き上げ、TikTokや、YouTubeのようなSNSを積極的に使ったことです。韓国アーティストのハイレベルなダンスはTikTokやYouTubeのダンスクリップで再生回数を急激に伸ばし、世界中の若者たちを瞬く間に魅了しました。またK-POPアイドルが国際的なアーティストとコラボしたり、英語や日本語を歌詞に取り入れたりしたことなども、J-POPよりも高い世界的な人気を得ることができた要因でした。

Part 4

On the other hand, J-Pop continues to be embraced by people around the world through its synergy with other popular aspects of Japanese visual culture, such as video games, anime, the aesthetics of "kawaii" and Akihabara fashion. Some recent American artists have had huge succes in teaming up with J-Pop artists. For example, "Mamushi," the collaboration between American Megan Thee Stallion and Japanese Yuki Chiba went viral in 2024. This type of song is a great example of globalization and could be the start of a new cultural wave for J-Pop.

Vocabulary and Expressions

PART 1

…年間 **...nenkan** for ... years

西洋 **seiyō** the West

爆発 **bakuhatsu** explosion

…的な **...teki na** suffix used to turn a noun into an adjective

成長 **seichō** growth

遂げる **togeru** to achieve

世界中 **sekaijū** worldwide

上位 **jōi** top rank

占める **shimeru** to occupy

一位 **ichi i** first place

獲得する **kakutoku suru** to obtain; to achieve

坂本九 **Sakamoto Kyū** Kyu Sakamoto (singer)

彼 **kare** he

曲 **kyoku** song

上を向いて歩こう **Ue o Muite Arukō** "Let's look up as we walk" (English title "Sukiyaki")

…年 **...nen** year ...(e.g., 1963, 2024)

邦楽 **hōgaku** Japanese music

要素 **yōso** element

音楽 **ongaku** music

Part 4

　一方、J-POPは、ビデオゲーム、アニメ、「かわいい」の美学、秋葉原のファッションなどの人気の高い日本のビジュアル文化との相乗効果を通じて、世界の人々に親しまれ続けています。最近のアメリカのアーティストの中には、J-POPアーティストとコラボし、人気を得ている人もいます。例えば、2024年のアメリカ人のミーガン・ジー・スタリオンと日本人の千葉雄喜のコラボ曲「Mamushi」は世界中で大ヒットしました。このような歌はグローバル化のよい例で、J-POPの新しい文化的な波の始まりかもしれません。

融合 **yūgō** fusion; blending

させる **saseru** to let ... do (causative form of する **suru** to do)

形成 **keisei** formation

…において **... ni oite** in ...; at ... (context or location)

重要な **jūyō na** important

礎 **ishizue** foundation

築く **kizuku** to build; to establish

PART 2

また **mata** again; also

…年代 **... nendai** decade (e.g., 1990年代, 1990s)

はじめ **hajime** beginning, start

東京 **Tōkyō** Tokyo

ジャニーズ事務所 **Janīzu Jimusho** Johnny & Associates

…という **...to iu** called ...

芸能プロダクション **geinō purodakushon** entertainment production company

誕生する **tanjō suru** to be born; to be formed

歌う **utau** to sing

踊れる **odoreru** to be able to dance (potential form of 踊る **odoru** to dance)

男性 dansei man; male

育成 ikusei training; nurturing

開始する kaishi suru to start; to begin

大変 taihen greatly

役立つ yakudatsu to be useful; to be helpful

例えば tatoeba for example

青写真 aojashin blueprint

述べる noberu to state; to mention

PART 3

大学 daigaku university

教授 kyōju professor

基 moto basis; foundation

発展する hatten suru to develop; to progress

違う chigau to be different

方向 hōkō direction

進む susumu to move forward

要因 yōin factor; cause

いくつか ikutsuka several, some

最も mottomo most

重要な jūyō na important

魅力 miryoku charm; appeal

高める takameru to enhance; to increase

まったく mattaku completely; totally

新しい atarashii new

引き上げる hikiageru to elevate; to raise

積極的に sekkyokuteki ni actively; positively

使う tsukau to use

韓国 Kankoku South Korea

再生回数 saisei kaisū number of views

急激に kyūgeki ni rapidly

伸ばす nobasu to increase

若者たち wakamonotachi young people

瞬く間に mataku ma ni in the blink of an eye, instantly

魅了する miryō suru to captivate; to fascinate

国際的な kokusaiteki na international

コラボする korabo suru to collaborate

(…た)り (...ta)ri to do ... and so on (following a verb in the ta-form)

英語 eigo English
日本語 nihongo Japanese
歌詞 kashi lyrics
取り入れる tori-ireru to incorporate; to adopt
高い takai high
世界 sekai world
人気 ninki popularity
得る eru to gain
…ことができる … koto ga dekiru to be able to … (following a verb in the dictionary form)

PART 4

一方 ippō on the other hand
美学 bigaku aesthetics
秋葉原 Akihabara Akihabara (district of Tokyo)
文化 bunka culture
相乗効果 sōjō kōka synergistic effect
…を通じて … o tsūjite through …
人々 hitobito people
親しまれる shitashimareru to be loved; to be well-liked
…続ける …tsuzukeru to continue …
最近 saikin recently
大ヒットする dai hitto suru to become a big hit
歌 uta song
グローバル化 gurōbaruka globalization
よい例 yoi rei good example
波 nami wave
始まり hajimari beginning
…かもしれない … kamo shirenai it may be …

Comprehension and Language

Select the most appropriate answer in the parentheses or fill in the gap.

1. K-POPはこの20年間、世界中のチャート（で・に）上位を占めている。

2. しかし、アメリカのビルボードではじめて一位を獲得したアジア人は（中国人・日本人）だった。

3. ジャニーズ事務所は1960年代にフォーリーブスやSMAPなどの（男性・女性）アイドルグループの育成をはじめ、J-POPの形成に役立った。

4. ジャニーズ事務所と（SMAP・フォーリーブス）はK-POPモデルの青写真を築いたと述べている人がいる。

5. しかし、K-POPのグループはビジュアル的な魅力を高め、ダンスをまったく新しいレベルに引き上げ、＿＿＿＿＿＿を積極的に使った。

6. またK-POPアイドルは国際的なアーティストとコラボしたり、英語や日本語を歌詞に取り入れ＿＿＿＿＿＿した。

7. 一方、J-POPは、日本の＿＿＿＿＿＿文化とのシナジーを通じて、世界の人々に親しまれ続けている。

8. 最近のアメリカのアーティストには、J-POPアーティストとコラボし、人気を得ている人もいる。J-POPの新しい波がはじまる（かも・よう）しれない。

Discussion Points

1. Which K-POP idols do you know best? What do you know about them?
2. Which J-POP idols do you know best? What do you know about them?
3. Do you think pop-music collaborations between artists from different countries can improve relationships between those countries? Give examples or reasons for your answer.

Ajia ongaku no gurōbaruka de wa K-Pop wa J-Pop ni katta no darō ka

Irezumi: Japan's Underground Tattoo Culture

by Brian Ashcraft

Award-winning author and Japan specialist Brian Ashcrafts takes a look into Japan's underground tattoo culture.

> **Key words**
>
> 入れ墨 **irezumi** tattoo
> 隠れる **kakureru** to hide (somewhere) (intransitive verb)
> 隠す **kakusu** to hide (something) (transitive verb)

Part 1

Although largely hidden, Japan's culture of *irezumi*—traditional tattoo art—remains strong. If you look closely, you'll catch glimpses. A glimpse of red under a sleeve. Some black at the edge of a pair of shorts. Flashes of yellow or blue. Irezumi are designed to be covered and worn under clothes. But because tattoos aren't out in the open in Japan as they are

入れ墨：
日本の隠れタトゥー文化
Irezumi: Nihon no kakure tatū bunka
ブライアン・アシュクラフト

Part 1

日本の伝統的な入れ墨文化は、表立っては見られないものの、今でも根強く残っています。よく目を凝らすと、袖口から赤い色が覗いていたり、短パンの裾から黒がちらりと見えたり、黄色や青が一瞬垣間見えたりすることもあります。これらの入れ墨は、あえて服の下に隠れるようにデザインされているのです。西洋ではタトゥーは見せるものですが、日本では隠すものです。だか

in the West, when you finally do see them, they have enormous impact and power. This is what makes irezumi unique; this is their appeal. Generally speaking, irezumi are personal and private, unlike Western-style tattoos, which often seem to be for show.

Part 2

In Japan, foreigners with tattoos are less likely to be judged harshly than the locals who have them. The common assumption is that Western-style tattoos are for fashion, while Japanese ones are for unsavory types. This is why inked celebrities like Johnny Depp or athletes like Brazilian soccer star Neymar Jr. can appear on television or in print ads with their tattoos on display.

Part 3

Meanwhile, many tattooed Japanese celebrities tend to cover their irezumi for fear of alienating fans or being misrepresented. Most people in Japan don't see tattoos during daily life. The chances of you seeing someone's irezumi at a PTA meeting, at a convenience store or McDonald's, or even on the subway, are very, very low.

らこそ、入れ墨を目にしたときに、そのインパクトや迫力を感じるのです。これが入れ墨の魅力であり、ユニークさです。一般的に、入れ墨は非常にプライベートなもので人前では見せず、見せることを前提とした西洋風のタトゥーとは異なります。

Part 2

日本では、外国人がタトゥーをしていても、日本人ほど厳しい目で見られることはあまりありません。西洋風のタトゥーはファッションとして捉えられる一方、日本のは好ましくないものだと見られがちです。だからこそ、ジョニー・デップのような有名人や、ブラジルのサッカー選手ネイマールのようなアスリートが、タトゥーを堂々と見せながらテレビや広告に出ることができるのです。

Part 3

一方、日本の有名人は、ファンを遠ざけたり誤解を招いたりすることを恐れて、入れ墨を隠すことが多いです。日本では、日常生活でタトゥーを目にする機会はほとんどなく、PTAの会議、コンビニやマクドナルド、さらには電車内などで他の人の入れ墨を見る可能性は非常に低いです。

Part 4

For all of that is made of irezumi's connection to Japanese organized crime, it's important to remember that, during the periods in which tattooers were persecuted and could be arrested for practicing their craft, it was the yakuza—Japan's mafia-like gangsters—who kept tattooers employed. Regardless of what you think of yakuza or their activities, if you like Japanese tattoos, the fact that yakuza have kept the tradition alive should be respected.

Vocabulary and Expressions

PART 1

伝統 **dentō** tradition

…的な **...teki na** suffix used to turn a noun into an adjective

入れ墨 **irezumi** tattoo

表立って **omotedatte** openly

見られる **mirareru** to be seen (passive of 見る to see)

…ものの **...monono** although …

今でも **ima demo** even now

根強く **nezuyoku** deeply rooted

残っている **nokotte iru** remaining

目を凝らす **me o korasu** to look closely

…と **... to** when …ing; after …ing (following a verb in the dictionary form)

袖口 **sodeguchi** sleeve opening

赤い **akai** red

色 **iro** color

覗く **nozoku** to peek

(…た) り **(... ta)ri** to do … etc. (following a verb in the **ta**-form)

短パン **tanpan** shorts

裾 **suso** hem

黒 **kuro** black

ちらりと **chirari to** fleetingly

見える **mieru** to be visible

Part 4

　入れ墨が日本の暴力団と関連しているという見方がある一方で、入れ墨師が迫害され、入れ墨を彫るだけで逮捕される恐れがあった時代に、彼らの仕事を支えていたのはヤクザ（日本のマフィア的な暴力団）だったことを忘れてはいけません。ヤクザやその活動に対する意見はさまざまでしょうが、日本の入れ墨文化が好きであれば、ヤクザがその伝統を守り続けてきたという事実に敬意を払うべきでしょう。

黄色 **kiiro** yellow

青 **ao** blue

一瞬 **isshun** moment

垣間見る **kaima miru** to glimpse

…ことがある **… koto ga aru** there are some occasions when … (following a verb in the plain non-past form)

あえて **aete** deliberately

服 **fuku** clothes

…の下に **… no shita ni** under …

隠れる **kakureru** to hide (somewhere); to be hidden

…ように **…yō ni** like … (following a verb in the plain form)

西洋 **seiyō** the West

見せる **miseru** to show

隠す **kakusu** to hide (something) (transitive verb)

だからこそ **dakara koso** precisely because

目にする **me ni suru** to see

…とき **… toki** at the time when …

迫力 **hakuryoku** intensity

感じる **kanjiru** to feel

魅力 **miryoku** charm, appeal

ユニークさ **yunīkusa** uniqueness

一般的に **ippanteki ni** generally

Irezumi: Nihon no kakure tatū bunka 87

非常に hijō ni extremely

人前 hito mae in front of people

見せず misezu not to show (short negative form of 見せる miseru to show)

前提 zentei premise

…風の ...fū no ...-style (suffix)

異なる kotonaru to differ

PART 2

外国人 gaikokujin foreigner

…でも ... demo even things like ... (following a noun)

厳しい目で見られる kibishii me de mirareru to be viewed critically

とらえられる toraerareru to be perceived (passive form of とらえる toraeru to perceive)

一方 ippō on the other hand

好ましい konomashii favorable

…がち ...gachi have a tendency to ...

だから ... dakara that's why ...; therefore ...

…こそ ... koso precisely ... (for emphasis)

有名人 yūmeijin celebrity

選手 senshu athlete

堂々と dōdō to without reservation; confidently

…ながら ...nagara while ...ing (following a verb in the stem form)

テレビ terebi television

広告 kōkoku advertisement

出る deru to appear

…ことができる ... koto ga dekiru to be able to ... (following a verb in the dictionary form)

PART 3

遠ざける tōzakeru to distance

誤解 gokai misunderstanding

招く maneku to invite; to cause

恐れる osoreru to fear

多い ōi many

日常生活 nichijō seikatsu daily life

目にする me ni suru to see; to witness

機会 kikai opportunity

会議 kaigi meeting

コンビニ konbini convenience store

電車 densha train

…内 ...nai inside ...

…など ... nado etc.; and so on

他の… **hoka no …** other …

可能性 **kanōsei** possibility

非常に **hijō ni** extremely

低い **hikui** low

PART 4

暴力団 **bōryokudan** crime syndicate

関連 **kanren** connection; association

見方 **mikata** perspective; viewpoint

入れ墨師 **irezumi-shi** tattoo artist

迫害 **hakugai** persecution

彫る **horu** to tattoo; to carve

…だけで **… dake de** just by …

逮捕 **taiho** arrest

…恐れ **… osore** risk of …; probability of … (following a verb in the plain non-past form)

時代 **jidai** era

彼らの **karera no** their

仕事 **shigoto** work; job

支える **sasaeru** to support

忘れる **wasureru** to forget

(…て) はいけない **(…te) wa ikenai** must not … (following a verb in the **te**-form)

活動 **katsudō** activity; activities

…に対する **… ni taisuru** toward …; regarding …

意見 **iken** opinion

さまざまな **samazama na** various

…でしょう **…deshō** I guess …

…が **… ga** but

好きな **suki na** fond of

…ば **…ba** if …; when … (**ba** conditional form of the verb)

守る **mamoru** to protect, to preserve

…続ける **…tsuzukeru** to continue … (following a verb in the stem form)

(…て) くる **…(te) kuru** to have been … (continuing action, following a verb in the **te**-form)

…という **…to iu** called …

事実 **jijitsu** fact; reality

敬意 **keii** respect

払う **harau** to pay (respect or money)

…べきだ **…beki da** should … (following a verb in the dictionary form)

Comprehension and Language

Select the most appropriate answer in the parentheses or fill in the gap.

1. 日本の伝統的な入れ墨文化は今でも残っているが、服の下に（隠れ・隠れる）ようにデザインされている。

2. 日本の有名人はテレビに出るときなどは入れ墨を（隠れる・隠す）。

3. これは見せることを前提とした（東洋・西洋）風のタトゥーとはちがう。

4. 日本では外国人は堂々とタトゥーを（見せ・見る）ながら日常生活をおくってもいいが、日本人はできない。

5. 日本では入れ墨は（暴力団・有名人）と関連していると思われがちだ。

6. 入れ墨師が迫害_____いた時代にヤクザは彼らの仕事を支えた。

7. 日本の入れ墨文化が好きであれば、ヤクザがその伝統を守り続けてきたという事実に敬意を（払う・払い）べきだ。

Discussion Points

1. Do you know anyone who has a tattoo? What is the design, and does it hold any particular meaning? Is it meant to be publicly seen or privately known?
2. Do you think Japanese people will adopt the Western-style perception of tattoos in the near future? Give a reason for your answer.
3. We learned that tattooing is perceived very differently depending on the social and historical context. Can you think of other examples of cultural practices that are viewed differently in different contexts?

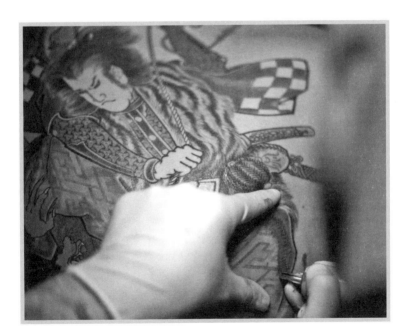

Japanese Women Break the Iron Ceiling

In official gender gap rankings, Japan continues to lag behind other advanced economies. Is this situation likely to change in the future?

> **Key words**
> 知事 **chiji** governor
> 代表取締役 **daihyō-torishimari-yaku** CEO
> 理事 **riji** board of directors

Part 1

In 2023, Japan ranked 125th in the Global Gender Gap Index from the World Economic Forum, the lowest in East Asia. This indicates that women in Japan face a persistent barrier. However, three Japanese females, Yuriko Koiko, Makiko Ono and Tokiko Shimizu, were recognized on the Forbes' 2023 list of the World's 100 Most Powerful Women, inspiring many other Japanese women.

鉄の天井を割る日本女性たち
Tetsu no tenjō o waru nihon joseitachi

Part 1

2023年、日本は世界経済フォーラム「グローバル・ジェンダー・ギャップ指数」で125位に落ち込み、東アジアで最も低い順位となりました。これは、日本の女性が直面する根深い障壁を意味します。しかし、2023年のフォーブス「世界で最も影響力のある女性100人」に、日本の小池百合子、小野真紀子、清水季子の三人が選ばれ、多くの日本女性にとって励みとなりました。

Part 2

Yuriko Koike is the first female governor of Tokyo. She was first elected governor in 2016 and re-elected in 2020 and 2024. She completed her bachelor's degree in sociology at Cairo University in Egypt and worked at Nippon TV, where she used her skills in Arabic to interview world leaders such as Yasser Arafat and Muammar Gaddafi. Upon receiving an Asia Game Changer Award in 2019, Koike said: "Hillary [Clinton] used the word 'glass ceiling' but in Japan, it isn't glass, it's an iron plate. I'm not Mrs. Thatcher, but what is needed is a strategy that advances a cause with conviction, clear policies and sympathy with the people."

Part 3

Makiko Ono is the first female CEO of Suntory Beverage and Food. She was appointed to this position in 2023. Ono studied Portuguese at Tokyo University of Foreign Studies, earned an executive MBA at the International Institute for Management Development (IMD) in Switzerland, and has held key leadership roles in Suntory's business in Europe. When she was appointed CEO, she said: "Career opportunities are now becoming fairer, so I hope that women will not give up and will seize whatever chances come their way."

Part 2

　小池百合子氏は、初の女性東京都知事です。2016年にはじめて知事に選ばれ、2020年と2024年に再選されました。小池氏はエジプトのカイロ大学で社会学の学士号を取得し、日本テレビに勤務し、そこでアラビア語の力を活かし、ヤーセル・アラファトやムアンマル・カダフィなどの世界のリーダーとのインタビューを行いました。2019年に「アジア・ゲームチェンジャー賞」を受賞した際に、小池氏はこう語りました。

　「ヒラリー（クリントン）は『ガラスの天井』という言葉を使いましたが、日本ではそれがガラスではなくて、鉄の板です。私はサッチャー夫人ではありませんが、信念をしっかり持ち、はっきりした政策を立て、人の気持ちを考えながら目標に向かい前進するための戦略を持つことは必要でしょう。」

Part 3

　小野真紀子氏は、サントリーフーズの初の女性代表取締役です。2023年にこの役職に着きました。小野氏は東京外国語大学でポルトガル語を学び、スイスのIMD（国際経営開発研究所）でエグゼクティブMBAを取得し、ヨーロッパでサントリーの重要なリーダーシップを発揮してきました。小野氏がCEOに就任した際、こう述べました。

　「キャリアの機会は今、公平になりつつあります。だからこそ、女性たちには決して諦めず、チャンスが来たらそれを掴んでほしいと思います。」

Part 4

Tokiko Shimizu served as the first female executive director of the Bank of Japan (BOJ) from May 2020 to May 2024. She was the first female executive director in the bank's 138-year history. She holds a bachelor's degree in urban engineering from the University of Tokyo and a master's degree in international policy from Stanford University. After her four-year term as executive director, her position was filled by a man, marking a return to an all-male leadership lineup at the BOJ and underscoring the ongoing challenges of achieving gender equality in leadership roles. In her first interview since leaving the BOJ in May 2024, Shimizu discussed her plans to launch her own consultancy, EmEco (short for Human Empowerment Ecosystem), aimed at increasing the participation of women in STEM-related fields, starting at the high school level. She said: "There are huge gaps between Japan and other countries; it's one of the main motivations for starting my new business. [...] Japanese women are not less talented than men. I can help fill that gap because women have a lot of potential."

Part 5

All three of these accomplished women have learned foreign languages, pursued higher education abroad and gained experience working internationally. These intercultural experiences must have broadened their horizons and given them the strength and confidence to begin challenging Japan's iron ceiling.

Part 4

　清水季子氏は、2020年5月から2024年5月まで、日本銀行（日銀）の理事を務めました。138年の日銀の歴史の中ではじめての女性理事でした。清水氏は東京大学で都市工学の学士号を、スタンフォード大学で国際政策学の修士号を取得しています。清水氏の4年間の理事の任期が終わった後、そのポジションは男性が引き継ぎ、日銀のリーダーシップは再び全員男性となり、リーダーシップにおける男女平等の達成がまだ難しいことが浮き彫りになりました。2024年5月に日銀を退職してからはじめてのインタビューで清水氏は、自身のコンサルタント会社「EmEco (Human Empowerment Ecosystem 人材強化エコシステムの略)」を立ち上げる計画について話しました。この会社は、高校レベルからSTEM関連分野で女性の参加を増やすことを目指しています。清水氏は次のように語りました。

　「日本と他の国との間にはまだ大きな差がありますが、それが新しいビジネスを始める主な動機の一つです。（中略）日本の女性は男性に劣っているわけではなく、女性はたくさんの可能性を持っていますから、私はその（男女の）差を埋める手助けができると思います。」

Part 5

　この三人の女性は皆、日本国外で別の言語を使って学び、働いた経験があります。これらの異文化間的な経験は彼女たちの視野を広げ、日本の女性に対する「鉄の天井」に挑む力と自信を与えたことに間違いありません。

Vocabulary and Expressions

PART 1

…年 ...nen year ...(e.g., 1963, 2023)

世界 sekai world

経済 keizai economy

指数 shisū index

…位 ...i rank

落ち込む ochikomu to fall; to decline

東アジア Higashi Ajia East Asia

最も mottomo most

低い hikui low

順位 jun'i rank

女性 josei women

直面する chokumen suru to face

根深い nebukai deep-rooted

障壁 shōheki barrier; obstacle

意味する imi suru to mean; to signify

影響 eikyō influence

…力 ...ryoku the power of ...

三人 sannin three people

選ばれる erabareru to be chosen (passive form of 選ぶ erabu to choose)

多くの ōku no many

…にとって ...ni totte for ... ; in terms of ...

励み hagemi encouragement

PART 2

…氏 ...shi honorific suffix used after someone's name

初の hatsu no first

東京都 Tōkyō-to Tokyo Metropolis

はじめて hajimete for the first time

知事 chiji governor

再選 saisen re-election

される sareru to be done ... (passive form of する suru to do)

大学 daigaku university

社会学 shakaigaku sociology

学士号 gakushigō bachelor's degree

取得する shutoku suru to obtain

勤務 kinmu employment

…語 ...go language (suffix)

力 chikara ability; power

活かす ikasu to make use of

行う okonau to carry out

…賞 ...shō ... award

受賞する jushō suru to be awarded

…際に ... sai ni on the occasion of ...; when ...

こう kō in this way; like this

語る kataru to speak; to talk

天井 tenjō ceiling

言葉 kotoba words, language

使う tsukau to use

鉄 tetsu iron

板 ita plate; board

…夫人 ...fujin Mrs. ...

信念 shinnen conviction

しっかり shikkari firmly

持つ motsu to hold; to have

はっきりした hakkiri shita clear

政策 seisaku policy

立てる tateru to establish, to make

人 hito person

気持ち kimochi feeling, emotion

考える kangaeru to think

…ながら ...nagara while ...ing (following a verb in the stem form)

目標 mokuhyō goal, objective

向かう mukau to head toward

前進する zenshin suru to move forward

…ための ... tame no for the purpose of ...

戦略 senryaku strategy

必要だ hitsuyō da to be necessary

PART 3

代表取締役 daihyō torishimari-yaku representative director, CEO

役職 yakushoku position; post

着く tsuku to assume; to take (a position)

東京外国語大学 Tōkyō Gaikokugo Daigaku Tokyo University of Foreign Studies

学ぶ manabu to study; to learn

国際 kokusai international

経営 keiei management

開発 kaihatsu development

研究所 kenkyūjo institute, research center

エグゼクティブ eguzekutibu executive

取得する shutoku suru to obtain; to acquire

重要な jūyō na important

発揮する hakki suru to demonstrate; to exhibit

就任する shūnin suru to assume office; to take up a post

述べる noberu to state; to mention

機会 kikai opportunity

今 ima now

公平 kōhei fairness; equality

…つつある …tsutsu aru (is) becoming … (following a verb in the stem form)

だからこそ dakara koso precisely because of this

決して kesshite by no means

諦めず akiramezu without giving up (a variation of the nai-form of 諦める akirameru to give up)

掴む tsukamu to grab; to seize

(…て)ほしい (…te) hoshii to want (someone) to (do something)

思う omou to think

PART 4

日本銀行（日銀）Nihon Ginkō (Nichigin) Bank of Japan (BOJ)

理事 riji executive director

務める tsutomeru to work, to serve

歴史 rekishi history

東京大学 Tōkyō Daigaku University of Tokyo

都市工学 toshi kōgaku urban engineering

学士号 gakushigō bachelor's degree

国際政策学 kokusai seisakugaku international policy studies

修士号 shūshigō master's degree

…年間 …nenkan for … years

任期 ninki term of office

終わる owaru to end; to finish

…後 … ato after … (following a verb in the ta-form)

男性 dansei man; male

引き継ぐ hikitsugu to take over; to succeed

再び futatabi again

全員 zen'in all members, entire group

…における … ni okeru regarding …

男女平等 danjo byōdō gender equality

達成 tassei attainment

難しい muzukashii difficult; challenging

浮き彫りになる ukibori ni naru to highlight; to bring to light

退職する **taishoku suru** to retire; to resign

自身の **jishin no** one's own; personal

コンサルタント会社 **konsarutanto-gaisha** consulting firm

人材 **jinzai** human resources

強化 **kyōka** strengthening

略 **ryaku** abbreviation

立ち上げる **tachiageru** to launch; to set up

計画 **keikaku** plan

…について **... ni tsuite** about ...

話す **hanasu** to talk; to speak

会社 **kaisha** company

高校 **kōkō** high school

関連 **kanren** related; relevant

分野 **bunya** field; area

参加 **sanka** participation

増やす **fuyasu** to increase

目指す **mezasu** to aim; to target

次のように **tsugi no yō ni** as follows

他の **hoka no** other

国 **kuni** country; nation

間 **aida** between; among

差 **sa** difference; gap

新しい **atarashii** new

主な **omona** main; primary

動機 **dōki** motive; motivation

一つ **hitotsu** one; single

中略 **chūryaku** omitted

劣っている **ototte iru** inferior; lagging behind

…わけではない **...wake de wa nai** it does not mean that ...

可能性 **kanōsei** possibility

埋める **umeru** to fill; to cover

手助け **tedasuke** help; assistance

できる **dekiru** to be able to

PART 5

皆 **mina** everyone; all

国外 **kokugai** overseas; abroad

別の **betsu no** different; separate

言語 **gengo** language

使う **tsukau** to use

働く **hataraku** to work

異文化間の **ibunkakan no** intercultural

…的な **...teki na** suffix used to turn a noun into an adjective

経験 **keiken** experience

彼女 **kanojo** she; her

…たち **...tachi** plural suffix for people and animals

視野 **shiya** field of vision; one's horizons

広げる **hirogeru** to broaden, to expand

…に対する **... ni taisuru** toward ...

挑む **idomu** to challenge; to tackle

自信 **jishin** confidence

与える **ataeru** to give; to provide

間違い **machigai** mistake; error

Comprehension and Language

Select the most appropriate answer in the parentheses or fill in the gap.

1. 日本のグローバル・ジェンダー・ギャップ指数はとても（低い・高い）。

2. しかし、2023年にフォーブスの「世界で最も影響力のある女性100人」に日本の女性が三人（選んだ・選ばれた）。

3. 小池百合子氏はエジプトの＿＿＿＿＿＿大学で社会学を勉強した。

4. 小池氏は東京都の初の女性の（社長・知事）だ。

5. 小池氏は、日本では女性はガラスの天井では（なくて・ないで）、鉄の板に直面していると言った。

6. 小野真紀子氏は＿＿＿＿＿＿でサントリーの重要なリーダーシップを発揮した。

7. 小野氏はサントリーの初の女性（理事・代表取締役）だ。

8. 清水季子氏は日銀の(138・38)年の歴史の中で、初の理事になった。

9. しかし、清水氏の任期が（終わった・終わる）後、そのポジションは男性が引継いだ。

10. 清水氏はSTEM関連分野で女性の参加を（増やす・減らす）ためのコンサルタント会社を作る計画をした。

Discussion Points

1. Do women face challenges in achieving leadership positions in your country? If so, what are some of the specific obstacles they encounter?

2. How can international exposure help Japanese college students develop leadership skills and broaden their worldview?

3. Do you think college students in your country should pursue global experiences? What are some benefits and challenges of studying or working abroad?

Why Are the Japanese So Bad at English?

According to the EF English Proficiency Index, Japan ranks much lower than South Korea and China in terms of English skills.

Key words

文法構造 **bunpō kōzō** grammatical structure
英会話スクール **eikaiwa sukūru** English conversation school
完璧主義 **kanpeki-shugi** perfectionism

Part 1

Japan ranked 87th in the global 2023 EF (Education First) English Proficiency Index, lower than most Asian countries, including South Korea (49th) and China (82nd). The Japanese government has been emphasizing the importance of English education for many decades, so why are the Japanese still so bad at English?

Part 2

Linguists might argue that the poor English skills of the Japanese are due to the significant difference between Japanese and English sentence structures. However, Korean sentence structures are quite similar to those of Japanese, so why does South Korea rank so much higher than Japan in English proficiency?

なぜ日本人は英語が苦手なのか？
Naze nihonjin wa eigo ga nigate na no ka

Part 1

2023年のEF英語能力指数で、日本は世界で87位と、多くのアジア諸国、たとえば韓国（49位）や、中国（82位）よりも低い順位でした。日本政府は何十年も前から英語教育を重要視してきましたが、なぜ日本人はまだ英語が苦手なのでしょうか？

Part 2

　言語学者は、日本人の英語力が低いのは、日本語と英語の文法構造が大きく異なるからだと主張するかもしれません。しかし、韓国語の文法構造は日本語と非常に似ていますが、韓国は日本よりもはるかに高い順位にあります。

Part 3

Others may attribute the poor English skills of the Japanese to their shyness and reserved demeanor. However, this perception holds true primarily when they are in the presence of their superiors during work hours. Once they start drinking at an izakaya after work, they can become loud and loquacious, even around those same superiors.

Part 4

Could it be that the Japanese simply don't like English? This seems unlikely, given the huge inventory of English loanwords that have entered the Japanese dictionary over the past century. There are so many English loanwords in Japanese that native English speakers learning Japanese might start wondering if they are studying Japanese or English!

Part 5

To add to the mystery, the Japanese seem eager to learn English. Many are willing to spend their own money to take *eikaiwa* (English conversation) lessons. Signs for eikaiwa schools can be seen posted everywhere throughout Japan.

Part 6

Then, why are the Japanese so bad at English? Perhaps their perfectionism and tendency to feel embarrassed makes them fearful of making mistakes. However, it's important to recognize that making errors while learning a new language is normal and nothing to be ashamed of.

Part 3
　他の人は、日本人の英語力の低さを、内向的で控えめな性格のせいだと考えるかもしれません。しかし、これは通常、勤務時間に上司と一緒にいるときだけ当てはまります。仕事が終わり、居酒屋で飲み始めると、その同じ上司がいても、声が大きくなり、途切れることなくしゃべりまくることがよくあります。

Part 4
　日本人は単に英語が嫌いなのでしょうか？しかし、それも違うでしょう。過去100年間に日本語辞書に取り入れられた英語の外来語は非常に多いです。英語の外来語があまりにも多いので、日本語を学んでいる英語ネイティブは自分は日本語を学んでいるのか、英語を学んでいるのかときどき分からなくなってしまいます。

Part 5
　さらに不思議なことに、日本人は英語を学びたいと強く思っているようです。多くの日本人は実費で英会話レッスンを受けていて日本のどこに行っても英会話スクールの看板が見えます。

Part 6
　では、なぜ日本人は英語が苦手なのでしょうか？日本人は完璧主義で、間違いを恐れているのかもしれません。しかし、新しい言語を使っているときに、間違いが生じることは普通のことで恥じることではありません。

Part 7

For the 2020 Tokyo Olympics and Paralympics, over 200,000 people applied to volunteer, helping to organize and assist thousands of foreign visitors around the city. Although it was not a mandatory qualification, the ability to speak English was expected. One of the applicants was a 90-year-old great-grandmother named Setsuko Takamizawa. She was determined to prove that it's never too late to learn English. Having been prevented from learning what used to be considered the "enemy language" in her youth during World War II, Takamizawa said: "We should live and act not only as Japanese but also as global citizens of the Earth."

This great-grandmother's determination to embrace the global stage far outweighs any fear of making mistakes.

Part 7

　2020年の東京オリンピックとパラリンピックでは、20万人以上の人々がボランティアに応募し、東京のあちこちでたくさんの外国人観光客をサポートすることになりました。必須条件ではありませんでしたが、英語を話せることが求められていました。応募者の一人に、90歳の曾おばあちゃんである高見澤摂子さんがいました。高見澤さんは「英語を学ぶのに遅すぎることはない」と証明したいと強く思い、英語を勉強しはじめました。高見澤さんが若い頃は第二次世界大戦中で英語は「敵国の言葉」とされ、学ぶことができなかったのです。高見澤さんはこう語りました。

　「わたしたちは日本人としてだけでなく、地球のグローバルな市民として生き、行動すべきです。」

　この曾おばあちゃんのグローバルな舞台に立とうとする決意は、間違いを恐れる気持ちをはるかに越えていました。

Vocabulary and Expressions

PART 1

…年 **...nen** year ...(e.g., 1963, 2025)

英語 **eigo** English

能力 **nōryoku** proficiency

指数 **shisū** index

世界 **sekai** world

…位 **...i** ...th place

多くの **ōku no** many

アジア諸国 **Ajia shokoku** Asian countries

たとえば **tatoeba** for example

韓国 **Kankoku** South Korea

中国 **Chūgoku** China

…より **... yori** than ...

低い **hikui** low

順位 **jun'i** ranking

政府 **seifu** government

何十年も **nanjūnen mo** for decades

前 **mae** ago

教育 **kyōiku** education

重要視する **jūyōshi suru** to emphasize; to prioritize

(…て) くる **(...te) kuru** to have been (doing) ... (following a verb in the **te**-form)

…が **...ga** ...; however (conjunction)

なぜ **naze** why

苦手な **nigate na** bad at; poor at

なぜ … のでしょうか **naze ... no deshō ka** Why is ...?; I wonder why ...

PART 2

言語学者 **gengogaku-sha** linguist

文法 **bunpō** grammar

構造 **kōzō** structure

大きく **ōkiku** significantly; greatly

異なる **kotonaru** to differ

…からだ **...kara da** It is because ...

主張する **shuchō suru** to claim; to assert

…かもしれない **... kamo shirenai** might ...; may ...

非常に **hijō ni** extremely

似ている **nite iru** to be similar

はるかに **haruka ni** far; much

高い **takai** high; tall

PART 3

他の **hoka no** other

…力 **...ryoku** ability to ...

低さ **hikusa** lowness

内向的な **naikōteki na** introverted

控えめな **hikaeme na** reserved

性格 **seikaku** personality

…のせいだ **... no sei da** due to ...; the fault of ...

考える **kangaeru** to think

通常 **tsūjō** usually; typically

勤務時間 **kinmu jikan** business hours

上司 **jōshi** boss; superior

…と一緒に **... to issho ni** together with ...

…とき **...toki** when ... (following a verb in the plain form)

…だけ **... dake** only ...

当てはまる **atehamaru** to be applicable

仕事 **shigoto** work; job

終わる **owaru** to end; to finish

居酒屋 **izakaya** izakaya (Japanese pub)

飲む **nomu** to drink

…始める **...hajimeru** to start ... (following a verb in the stem form)

…と **... to** when ...ing; after ...ing (following a verb in the dictionary form)

同じ **onaji** same

(…て)も **(...te) mo** even if ... (following a verb in the **te**-form)

声 **koe** voice

大きくなる **ōkiku naru** to get louder

途切れる **togireru** to be interrupted

…ことなく **... koto naku** without ...

しゃべる **shaberu** to talk; to chat

…まくる **...makuru** to do something excessively (following a verb in the stem form)

…ことがある **... koto ga aru** there are times when ... (following a verb in the plain non-past form)

PART 4

単に **tan ni** simply

嫌いだ **kirai da** to dislike

違う **chigau** to differ; to be different

…のでしょうか **...no deshō ka** could it be that ...?

過去 **kako** the past

…年間 **...nenkan** for ... years

辞書 **jisho** dictionary

取り入れられる **tori-irerareru** to be incorporated (passive form of 取り入れる **tori-ireru** to incorporate)

外来語 **gairaigo** loanword

多い **ōi** many; numerous

あまりにも **amarini mo** too much; excessively

…ので **...node** because ...

学ぶ **manabu** to learn

自分 **jibun** oneself

分からない **wakaranai** to not understand (**nai**-form of 分かる **wakaru** to understand)

(…て)しまう **(... te) shimau** to end up ...; to do (something) completely (following a verb in the **te**-form)

PART 5

さらに **sara ni** furthermore; additionally

不思議な **fushigi na** mysterious; strange

…たい **...tai** to want to ... (following a verb in the stem form)

強く **tsuyoku** strongly

思う **omou** to think; to feel

…ようだ **...yō da** it appears that ...

多くの **ōku no** many

実費で **jippi de** at one's own expense

英会話 **eikaiwa** English conversation

受ける **ukeru** to take (a lesson); to receive

どこに行っても **doko ni itte mo** wherever one goes

看板 **kanban** signboard

見える **mieru** to be visible

PART 6

完璧主義 **kanpeki-shugi** perfectionism

間違い **machigai** mistake

恐れる **osoreru** to fear

…かもしれない **... kamo shirenai** it is possible that ...

新しい **atarashii** new

言語 **gengo** language

使う **tsukau** to use

生じる **shōjiru** to occur; to arise

普通 **futsū** normal; ordinary

恥じる **hajiru** to be ashamed

PART 7

20万人 (まんにん) **20 man-nin** 200,000 people

…以上 (いじょう) **...ijō** more than ...

人々 (ひとびと) **hitobito** people

応募する (おうぼ) **ōbo suru** to apply

あちこち **achikochi** here and there

外国人 (がいこくじん) **gaikokujin** foreigner

観光客 (かんこうきゃく) **kankō-kyaku** tourist

…ことになる **... koto ni naru** to be decided that ...

必須条件 (ひっすじょうけん) **hissu-jōken** prerequisite

話せる (はな) **hanaseru** to be able to speak (potential form of 話す **hanasu** to speak)

求められる (もと) **motomerareru** to be required (passive form of 求める **motomeru** to seek to)

…者 **...sha** (suffix) person associated with a particular role

一人 (ひとり) **hitori** one person

…歳 (さい) **...sai** ... years old

曾おばあちゃん (ひい) **hī-obāchan** great-grandmother

遅い (おそ) **osoi** late; slow

…すぎる **...sugiru** too ...; excessively ... (following a verb or an adjective in the stem form)

証明する (しょうめい) **shōmei suru** to prove

勉強する (べんきょう) **benkyō suru** to study

…はじめる **...hajimeru** to start ...; to begin ...(following a verb in the stem form)

若い (わか) **wakai** young

…頃 (ころ) **...koro** time period when ...

第二次世界大戦 (だいにじせかいたいせん) **dai-niji-sekai-taisen** World War II

…中 (ちゅう) **...chū** during ...

敵国 (てきこく) **tekikoku** enemy country

言葉 (ことば) **kotoba** language; word

できなかった **dekinakatta** could not do

こう **kō** in this way; like this

語る (かた) **kataru** to speak; to tell

…として **...toshite** as ...; in the role of ...

…だけでなく **... dake de naku** not only ...

地球 (ちきゅう) **chikyū** the Earth

市民 (しみん) **shimin** citizen

生きる (い) **ikiru** to live

行動する (こうどう) **kōdō suru** to act

…べきだ **...beki da** should; ought to (following a verb in the dictionary form)

すべきだ **subeki da** should do; ought to do (abbreviation of するべきだ **suru beki da**)

舞台 **butai** stage

立とう **tatō** let (me/us) stand (volitional form of 立つ **tatsu** to stand)

(…よう) とする **(...yō) to suru** to try to … (following a verb in the volitional form)

決意 **ketsui** determination; resolve

気持ち **kimochi** feeling; emotion

越える **koeru** to exceed; to surpass

Comprehension and Language

Select the most appropriate answer in the parentheses or fill in the gap.

1. 日本の英語能力の順位は韓国や中国などの多くの＿＿＿＿＿＿＿＿ 諸国より低い。

2. 韓国語と日本語の文法構造は非常に（違う・似ている）が、韓国の英語能力のランクは日本のよりとても高い。

3. 日本人の英語能力の低さは内向的で控えめな性格の（せい・おかげ）だと言う人もいるが、そうでもないようだ。

4. 日本人は英語が嫌いなのでもない。日本語辞書には英語の外来語がたくさん取り入れ（て・られて）いる。

5. 日本人は英語を学びたくないのでもない。多くの日本人は実費（に・で）英会話のレッスンを受けている。

6. 日本人は完璧主義で間違いを恐れているのかも（しれない・しれる）。

7. しかし、新しい言語を使っているときに、間違いが生じることは普通で恥じる（べきだ・べきではない）。

8. 曾おばあさんの高見澤さんは東京オリンピック・パラリンピックのボランティアに応募し、英語を勉強し（はじめた・すぎた）。

9. 高見澤さんは「英語を学ぶのに（遅・遅く）すぎることはない。」と言った。

Discussion Points

1. How do you feel if you make a mistake when speaking a foreign language?
2. Do you feel embarrassed when your pronunciation differs from that of native speakers? Why/why not?
3. How do you feel when non-native English speakers speak with an accent?

Japan's High Suicide Rate

Why does Japan have such a high suicide rate? Is it because of the country's history of seppuku and kamikaze? Is it because of social pressure? Or is it because of the stigma around getting therapy?

Key words

過労 **karō** overwork

経済不況 **keizai fukyō** economic downturn

恥 **haji** shame

Part 1

In 2016, a twenty-four-year-old woman, who graduated from a top-tier Japanese university and was employed by a top-tier Japanese company, committed suicide due to overwork. The company had a culture of relentless long hours that demanded excellence without compromise from its employees. The woman texted her friends and her mother more than fifty times during the two months before she committed suicide. Some of her messages read, "The materials I worked on during my day off were harshly criticized. My body and mind are completely shattered," and "I've lost all emotions except the desire to sleep." Her messages also indicated possible power harassment by her superior.

日本の高い自殺率
Nihon no takai jisatsuritsu

Part 1

2016年、日本の一流大学を卒業し、一流会社に就職した24歳の女性が過労で自殺しました。その会社には過酷な長時間労働の風習があり、従業員には妥協を許さない完璧さが求められていました。女性は自殺する前の2ヶ月間、友人や母親に50回以上のメッセージを送っていました。その中には、「休日返上で作った資料をぼろくそに言われた。もう体も心もズタズタだ」とか、「眠りたい以外の感情を失った」といった内容が含まれていました。また、上司によるパワハラの可能性を示すようなメッセージもありました。

Part 2

Sadly, this kind of story is not unusual in Japan. According to the Organization for Economic Co-operation and Development, the suicide rate in Japan in 2020 was the highest among G7 countries (0.015 percent), followed by the United States (0.014 percent). In a culture where honor, loyalty, saving face and self-sacrifice have for centuries been regarded as virtues, as seen in samurai seppuku rituals and kamikaze suicide attacks, the desire to avoid perceived shame can sometimes lead individuals to view suicide as a preferable option, especially during periods of economic downturn.

Part 3

Other serious factors that contribute to suicide today include social pressure and bullying. The intense pressure to succeed academically and professionally and to conform to societal expectations can lead to significant stress. When individuals feel they are unable to meet these expectations, it can result in feelings of inadequacy, which may contribute to suicidal thoughts. Highly accomplished individuals, like the woman mentioned earlier, often find themselves trapped by social pressures.

Part 2

　残念ながら、このような話は日本では珍しくありません。経済協力開発機構によると、2020年の日本の自殺率はG7諸国の中で一番高く(0.015%)、次はアメリカ(0.014%)でした。名誉、忠誠、体面、そして犠牲を重んじることが何世紀にもわたって美徳とされてきた文化では、武士の切腹や神風特攻が行われてきました。こうした背景の中で、特に経済不況のときに、恥を避けるために自殺がより良い選択肢と見なされることがあるのです。

Part 3

　また、今では社会的なプレッシャーやいじめも自殺につながることがあります。学業や仕事で成功し、社会の期待に応えるという強いプレッシャーが、大きなストレスを引き起こすことがあります。これらの期待に応えられないと感じたとき、劣等感を抱き、それが自殺を考える一因になることもあります。上記の女性のように、非常に優秀な人たちは、しばしば社会的なプレッシャーに囚われてしまいます。

Part 4

In Western cultures, the practice of seeking help from professional therapists is normal; however, in Japan and some other Asian countries, many people are reluctant to seek professional help for many reasons, including fear of social stigma. The Asian stigma extends across oceans; the number of Asian Americans are seeking therapy has increased recently thanks to heightened awareness of mental health issues during the COVID-19 pandemic, but Asian Americans are still significantly less likely to utilize mental health services compared to their non-Asian counterparts. Clinical psychologist Andrew Grimes, who established the office Tokyo Counseling Services in 1999, says: "There has got to be a shift away from the old mentality. [...] People must be able to go for mental healthcare without it affecting the image they have at work."

Part 5

In addition, it is essential that every institution makes it a top priority to create environments that are completely free from harassment and bullying. It should be the responsibility and a key qualification of managers and administrators to be able to support those who work for them. We can all help make this a reality within our circles by being advocates, allies and takers of action.

Part 4
　欧米では、精神的な問題は専門のセラピストに相談するのが一般的ですが、日本や他のアジア諸国では周りの人から社会的偏見を持たれるのを恐れて専門的な助けを求めないことが多いです。アジアにおけるスティグマは海を越えて広がっています。アジア系アメリカ人がセラピーを受けることは、コロナパンデミック中の心の健康状態に対する意識の高まりによって最近改善しました。しかし、それでもまだ大きな障壁があります。アジア系以外の人々と比べてアジア系アメリカ人が心の健康を保つためのサービスを利用する可能性はかなり低いままなのです。1999年に東京カウンセリングサービスを設立したアンドリュー・グライムズ氏はこう述べています。
　「古い考え方からの転換が必要です。(中略)職場での評価に影響を与えず、精神的なケアを受けられる環境を整えることが必要です。」

Part 5
　さらに、すべての組織や企業はハラスメントやいじめのない環境を作ることを最優先にすべきです。経営者や管理職にとって、働く人たちをサポートすることは責任であり、それができることが重要な資格であるべきです。わたしたち各自が擁護者、味方、そして行動を起こす者になり、身近なところからこれを実現していくことができるはずです。

Vocabulary and Expressions

PART 1

…年 ...nen year ...(e.g., 1963, 2016)
一流 ichiryū top-tier; prestigious
大学 daigaku university
卒業する sotsugyō suru to graduate
会社 kaisha company
就職する shūshoku suru to be employed at (a company)
…歳 ...sai ... years old
女性 josei woman
過労 karō overwork
自殺 jisatsu suicide
過酷な kakoku na harsh; severe
長時間労働 chō jikan rōdō long working hours
風習 fūshū custom
従業員 jūgyōin employee
妥協 dakyō compromise
許さない yurusanai does not allow (nai-form of 許す yurusu to allow)
完璧さ kanpekisa perfectionism; perfection
求められる motomerareru to be required; to be demanded
前 mae before
2ヶ月間 nikagetsukan for two months
友人 yūjin friend
母親 hahaoya mother
50回 gojukkai 50 times
…以上 ...ijō more than ...
送る okuru to send
休日 kyūjitsu holiday; day off
休日返上 kyūjitsu henjō working on a day off
作る tsukuru to create; to make
資料 shiryō materials; documents
ぼろくそに borokuso ni harshly; severely (criticized)
言われる iwareru to be told
体 karada body
心 kokoro mind; heart
ズタズタだ zutazuta da to be shattered; to be torn apart
…とか ...toka such as ...; or ...
眠る nemuru to sleep
…たい ...tai to want to ... (following a verb in the stem form)

…以外 … igai except for …

感情 kanjō emotions

失う ushinau to lose

内容 naiyō content

含まれる fukumareru to be included

上司 jōshi boss; superior

…による … ni yoru because of …; by …

パワハラ pawahara power harassment

可能性 kanōsei possibility; potential

示す shimesu to indicate; to show

…ような …yō na like … (following a verb in the plain form)

PART 2

残念 zannen unfortunate; regrettable

…ながら …nagara while …; although …

話 hanashi story; situation

珍しい mezurashii rare; unusual

経済協力開発機構 Keizai Kyōryoku Kaihatsu Kikō Organization for Economic Co-operation and Development (OECD)

…によると … ni yoru to according to …

…率 …ritsu …rate

諸国 shokoku countries

一番 ichiban most, first

高い takai high

次 tsugi next

名誉 meiyo honor

忠誠 chūsei loyalty

体面 taimen reputation; saving face

犠牲 gisei sacrifice

重んじる omonjiru to value or respect

何世紀にもわたって nanseiki ni mo watatte over many centuries

美徳 bitoku virtue

…とされる …to sareru to be considered …; to be regarded as …

文化 bunka culture

武士 bushi samurai

切腹 seppuku seppuku ritual suicide

神風特攻 kamikaze tokkō kamikaze suicide mission

行(おこな)われる **okonawareru** to be carried out (passive form of 行う **okonau** to carry out)

(…て) くる **(...te) kuru** has been (continuing to) …

背景(はいけい) **haikei** background

特(とく)に **toku ni** especially

経済不況(けいざいふきょう) **keizai fukyō** economic downturn

恥(はじ) **haji** shame

避(さ)ける **sakeru** to avoid

…ために **...tame ni** in order to …; for the sake of …

より良(よ)い **yori yoi** better

選択肢(せんたくし) **sentakushi** option; choice

見(み)なされる **minasareru** to be regarded as; to be considered (passive form of 見なす **minasu** to consider)

…ことがある **... koto ga aru** there are times when … (following a verb in the plain non-past form)

PART 3

今日(こんにち)では **kon'nichi dewa** nowadays

社会(しゃかい) **shakai** society

…的(てき)な **...teki na** suffix used to turn a noun into an adjective

いじめ **ijime** bullying

つながる **tsunagaru** to connect; to be linked

学業(がくぎょう) **gakugyō** studies; academics

仕事(しごと) **shigoto** work; job

成功(せいこう)する **seikō suru** to succeed

期待(きたい) **kitai** expectation

応(こた)える **kotaeru** to meet; to respond to

強(つよ)い **tsuyoi** strong

大(おお)きな **ōki na** big; large

引(ひ)き起(お)こす **hikiokosu** to cause; to bring about

感(かん)じる **kanjiru** to feel

…とき **...toki** when … (following a verb in the plain form)

劣等感(れっとうかん) **rettōkan** inferiority complex

抱(いだ)く **idaku** to embrace

考(かんが)える **kangaeru** to think; to consider

一因(いちいん) **ichi'in** one of the causes; a contributing factor

上記(じょうき)の **jōki no** mentioned above

…のように **... no yō ni** (just) like … (following a noun)

非常に hijō ni extremely

優秀な yūshū na excellent; outstanding

…たち ...tachi plural suffix for people and animals

しばしば shibashiba often; frequently

囚われる torawareru to be trapped; to be caught

(…て) しまう (... te) shimau to end up ...ing (following a verb in the te-form)

PART 4

精神的な seishinteki na mental

欧米 Ōbei Western countries (Europe and North America)

専門の senmon no specialized; professional

相談する sōdan suru to consult; to seek advice

一般的な ippanteki na general; common

アジア諸国 Ajia shokoku Asian countries

周りの… mawari no ... surrounding ...

偏見を持たれる henken o motareru to be prejudiced against

恐れる osoreru to fear

助け tasuke help; assistance

求める motomeru to seek; to ask for

多い ōi many; numerous

海を越える umi o koeru to cross the ocean

広がる hirogaru to spread

アジア系アメリカ人 Ajia-kei Amerikajin Asian American

受ける ukeru to receive

心 kokoro mind; heart

健康 kenkō health

状態 jōtai state

…に対する ... ni taisuru toward ...

意識の高まり ishiki no takamari increased awareness

…によって ni yotte by ...

最近 saikin recently

改善する kaizen suru to improve

障壁 shōheki barrier

…以外 ... igai other than ...

…と比べて ...to kurabete compared to ...

保つ tamotsu to maintain; to keep

利用する riyō suru to utilize

可能性 kanōsei possibility

低い hikui low

…ままだ ...mama da still remains ...

設立する setsuritsu suru to establish; to found

…氏 ...shi honorific suffix used after someone's name

こう kō in this way; like this

述べる noberu to state; to mention

古い furui old

考え方 kangaekata way of thinking

転換 tenkan shift; change

必要だ hitsuyō da necessary

中略 chūryaku omitted

職場 shokuba workplace

評価 hyōka evaluation

影響 eikyō influence; impact

与えず ataezu without giving (short form of the nai-form of 与える ataeru to give)

受けられる ukerareru to be able to receive (potential form of 受ける ukeru to receive)

環境 kankyō environment

整える totonoeru to arrange properly

PART 5

さらに sara ni furthermore; additionally

すべての… subete no ... all ...; every ...

組織 soshiki organization

企業 kigyō company

いじめ ijime bullying; harassment

作る tsukuru to create

最優先 saiyūsen top priority

…べきだ ...beki da should ...; ought to ... (following a verb in the dictionary form)

すべきだ subeki da should do; ought to do (abbreviation of するべきだ)

経営 keiei business management

…者 ...sha (suffix) person associated with a particular role

管理職 kanrishoku management position

…にとって ... ni totte for ...; in terms of ...

働く hataraku to work

責任 sekinin responsibility

できる dekiru to be able to

重要な jūyō na important

資格 shikaku qualification; competency

各自 kakuji each person

支持者 shiji-sha supporter

味方 mikata ally

行動 kōdō action

起こす okosu to initiate (an action)

者 mono person

身近なところ mijika na tokoro within one's circle; nearby

実現する jitsugen suru to accomplish

(…て) いく (...te) iku to continue to do (following a verb in the **te**-form)

…はずだ **...hazu da** is supposedly the case that ...

Comprehension and Language

Select the most appropriate answer in the parentheses or fill in the gap.

1. この数十年間の日本での自殺率は他のG7諸国と比較して（高い・低い）。

2. 日本での経済不況の他に、日本の伝統的（な・の）名誉の文化も要因の一つだ。

3. 日本では「名誉」や「体面」を保つことが美徳（と・で）されている。

4. それが保てないときには、＿＿＿＿＿を避けるために自殺を考える人もいる。

5. また、社会的なプレッシャーも自殺につながること（を・が）ある。

6. 非常に優秀な人たちは、しばしば社会的なプレッシャーに囚われて（しまう・おく）。

7. 精神的な問題は欧米では専門の＿＿＿＿＿＿＿に相談することが一般的だが、日本や他のアジア諸国ではあまりない。

8. セラピストに会うと、職場などで＿＿＿＿＿＿＿をもたれると考えられているからだ。

9. 日本でも人々が職場での評価に影響を与えられ（て・ず）精神的なケアを受けられる環境を整えることが必要だ。

10. また、経営者や管理職の人はハラスメントやいじめの（ある・ない）環境を作ることを最優先にすべきだ。

Discussion Points

1. Describe an incidence of bullying you have experienced or witnessed.
2. What policies does your school or workplace have to address and prevent bullying?
3. How do you think we can support or help those who feel pressure to achieve high performance in their studies or jobs?

Transforming Japan's Way of Working

Loyalty to the workplace is important in Japan, where lifetime employment is still common, as is excessive overtime. Will Japan's working practices change?

Key words

残業 **zangyō** overtime

年功序列 **nenkō-joretsu** seniority-based system

外資系企業 **gaishikei kigyō** foreign-owned company

Part 1

In the latter half of the twentieth century, Japan's economy was supported by unique employment practices deeply rooted in the culture, such as lifetime employment, overtime work, a seniority-based promotion system and limited vacation time. These practices helped Japan become a global economic powerhouse. However, since the bubble economy burst at the end of the twentieth century, base salaries have stagnated. Many young Japanese people are now showing interest in foreign-owned *gaishikei* companies operating within Japan, which tend to adopt more international working practices rather than traditional Japanese ones.

変わりゆく働き方のカタチ
Kawari yuku hatarakikata no katachi

Part 1

20世紀後半、日本の経済は終身雇用、残業、年功序列、そして少ない休暇といった深く日本文化に根付いた独自の雇用慣習によって支えられていました。これらの慣習は、日本が世界的な経済大国として成長するのに大変役立ちました。しかし、20世紀末のバブル経済崩壊以降、日本の基本給は停滞しています。今、若い日本人の間で、国内の外資系企業への関心が高まっています。外資系企業では、従来の日本的な雇用慣習でなく、国際的な雇用慣習を採用していることが多いからです。

Part 2

Ayako is one of them. She is a software engineer looking for a new job, who says, "I want a career that values my skills and contributions." Higher salaries and merit-based promotions are significant draws for her. Other attractive features are less overtime, reduced discrimination based on gender and age, and a more balanced and comfortable work environment.

Part 3

Kenji, a marketing manager at a foreign-owned consulting agency, says, "I love the freedom I have in this company to innovate and express my opinions." According to him, the company's flat culture—an organizational system where hierarchy is minimized—has created a collaborative environment where fresh ideas flow freely and open discussions are encouraged.

Part 4

However, working for a foreign-owned company is not without its challenges. Makoto, a recent graduate, says: "The frequent changes in personnel make me feel anxious. I'm also worried that the company's global strategy might lead it to withdrawing from Japan." He is concerned, too, that the intense focus on achieving high performance, while motivating, may also be a source of stress.

Part 2

　その一人は彩子さんです。彩子さんはソフトウェアエンジニアで、今、新しい職を探しています。彩子さんは「自分の技能や貢献を評価してくれる仕事を希望しています」と話しています。彩子さんにとって、高い給与や実力主義の昇進が大きな魅力です。また、残業が少なく、性別や年齢による差別が少ないこと、よりバランスの取れた働きやすい環境も魅力です。

Part 3

　また、外資系コンサルティング会社でマーケティングマネージャーを務める研治さんは、「この会社では自由に意見を出し、新しいことに挑戦できるのが気に入っています」と述べています。彼によれば、この会社のフラットな文化—上下関係をできるだけ少なくした組織体制—は、斬新なアイデアが活発に飛び交い、自由に議論できる協力的な環境を築いているとのことです。

Part 4

　しかし、外資系企業で働くことには課題もあります。新卒の誠さんは、「人事異動が頻繁にあるのが気になります。また、グローバル戦略の影響で会社が日本から撤退する可能性があることも不安です」と話しています。さらに、高いパフォーマンスを求められることが、やる気を引き出す一方で、ストレスの原因にもなる可能性があると懸念しています。

Kawari yuku hatarakikata no katachi

Part 5

Young people's interest in foreign-owned companies also presents an opportunity for Japanese companies to reform their structures to attract motivated Japanese workers. Finding a balance between traditional employment practices and new ways of working will be crucial for Japan's sustained economic development.

Vocabulary and Expressions

PART 1

世紀 **seiki** century
後半 **kōhan** latter half
経済 **keizai** economy
終身雇用 **shūshin koyō** lifetime employment
残業 **zangyō** overtime work
年功序列 **nenkō joretsu** seniority system
少ない **sukunai** few
休暇 **kyūka** vacation; day off
深く **fukaku** deeply
文化 **bunka** culture
根付いた **nezuita** rooted
独自 **dokujī** unique
雇用慣習 **koyō kanshū** employment practices

…によって **... ni yotte** by …
支えられる **sasaerareru** to be supported (passive form of 支える **sasaeru** to support)
世界 **sekai** world
…的な **…teki na** suffix used to turn a noun into an adjective
経済大国 **keizai taikoku** economic superpower
…として **…toshite** as …
成長する **seichō suru** to grow
大変 **taihen** very; greatly
役立つ **yakudatsu** to be useful
末 **sue** end
バブル経済 **baburu keizai** bubble economy
崩壊 **hōkai** collapse
…以降 **… ikō** after …; since …

若者が外資系企業に関心を持つことは、日本企業にとっても、雇用慣習を改革し、意欲的な日本人の働き手を集めるいい機会となります。伝統的な働き方と新しい働き方のバランスを見つけることが、日本の持続可能な経済成長にとって重要になるでしょう。

基本給 **kihon-kyū** base salary
停滞する **teitai suru** to stagnate
今 **ima** now
若い **wakai** young
…の間 **... no aida** during ...
国内 **kokunai** domestic
外資系 **gaishikei** foreign-owned
企業 **kigyō** company
関心 **kanshin** interest
高まる **takamaru** to increase
従来の… **jūrai no ...** traditional ...
採用する **saiyō suru** adopt
多い **ōi** many

PART 2

一人 **hitori** one person
新しい **atarashii** new

職 **shoku** job
探す **sagasu** to search
自分 **jibun** oneself
技能 **ginō** skills
貢献 **kōken** contribution
評価する **hyōka suru** to evaluate
仕事 **shigoto** work; job
希望する **kibō suru** to hope; to wish
話す **hanasu** to speak
…にとって **... ni totte** for ...; in terms of ...
高い **takai** high
給与 **kyūyo** salary
実力主義 **jitsuryoku-shugi** meritocracy
昇進 **shōshin** promotion

魅力 miryoku attraction

性別 seibetsu gender

年齢 nenrei age

差別 sabetsu discrimination

バランスの取れた baransu no toreta balanced

働く hataraku to work

…やすい …yasui easy to … (following a verb in the stem form)

環境 kankyō environment

PART 3

会社 kaisha company

務める tsutomeru to work for

自由に jiyū ni freely

意見を出す iken o dasu to express an opinion

挑戦する chōsen suru to challenge; to try

できる dekiru to be able

気に入る ki ni iru to like; to be pleased with

述べる noberu to state; to mention

彼 kare he

…によれば … ni yoreba according to …

上下関係 jōge kankei hierarchical relationship

できるだけ dekiru dake as much as possible

組織体制 soshiki taisei organizational structure

斬新な zanshin na innovative

活発に kappatsu ni actively

飛び交う tobikau to fly around; to be in the air

自由に jiyū ni freely

議論する giron suru to discuss

協力 kyōryoku cooperation

環境 kankyō environment

築く kizuku to build; to establish

PART 4

課題 kadai issue; challenge

新卒 shinsotsu new graduate

人事異動 jinji idō personnel transfer

頻繁に hinpan ni frequently

気になる ki ni naru to be concerned about

戦略 senryaku strategy

影響 eikyō influence; impact

撤退する tettai suru to withdraw

可能性 kanōsei possibility

不安な fuan na uneasy; anxious

求められる motomerareru to be demanded to (passive form of 求める motomeru to seek to; to demand)

やる気 yaruki motivation

引き出す hikidasu to draw out; to bring out

一方で ippō de on the other hand

原因 gen'in cause

懸念する kenen suru to be concerned; to worry

PART 5

若者 wakamono young people

持つ motsu to have; to hold

改革する kaikaku suru to reform

意欲 iyoku ambition

働き手 hatarakite worker

集める atsumeru to gather

機会 kikai opportunity

伝統 dentō tradition

働き方 hatarakikata way of working

新しい atarashii new

見つける mitsukeru to find

持続可能な jizoku kanō na sustainable

経済成長 keizai seichō economic growth

重要 jūyō important

…でしょう …deshō I guess …

Comprehension and Language

Select the most appropriate answer in the parentheses or fill in the gap.

1. 20世紀後半の日本の経済は終身雇用、残業、年功＿＿＿＿、少ない休暇などによって支えられ、日本は経済大国になった。

2. しかし、20世紀末のバブル経済＿＿＿＿以降、日本の基本給は低いままだ。

3. 今、日本の若者は国内の＿＿＿＿企業に関心をもっている。

4. 彩子さんは給与が高く、昇進は実力主義、残業が少なく、＿＿＿＿や年齢による差別が少ないことなどが外資系企業の魅力だと思っている。

5. 研治さんはフラットな組織体制で、自由に＿＿＿＿を出し、協力しながら、新しいことに挑戦できることなどが、外資系企業の魅力だと考えている。

6. しかし、誠さんは＿＿＿＿異動が頻繁にあること、日本から撤退する可能性があること、実力主義はやる気が出てもストレスの原因になる可能性があることなどが、外資系企業の難しいところだと思っている。

7. 伝統的な働き方と新しい働き方のバランスを見つけることが、日本の持続可能な経済成長に（よって・とって）重要になるだろう。

Discussion Points

1. What do you think are the pros and cons of lifetime employment for the employer and employee?
2. What factors do you believe have contributed to the decline in the performance of Japanese companies over the last few decades?
3. Do you find a focus on achieving a high performance motivating or stressful? Give reasons for your answer.

Japan's Drinking Culture
by Chris Bunting

Japanese company employees look serious and quiet during business hours but present a completely different personality at izakaya bars after work.

> **Key words**
> 乾杯！ **Kanpai!** Cheers!
> お酌 **o-shaku** pouring sake into others' glasses
> 本音 **honne** true feelings (or honest feelings)

Part 1

Kampai!

Many Japanese drinking sessions will start with a toast and it is polite not to start gulping until the customary loud chorus of *kampai!* Another drinking exclamation is *banzai!*, which is far less popular than it once was but is still occasionally heard close to the climax of an evening, particularly at company parties. *Banzai* does not mean that everybody

日本の飲み文化
Nihon no nomi bunka
クリス・バンティング

Part 1
乾杯！

日本の飲み会はたいてい乾杯で始まります。そして、大きな声で皆そろって「乾杯！」と叫ぶまでは、飲みはじめないのが礼儀です。もう一つの飲みはじめの言葉に「万歳！」がありますが、昔ほど人気はありません。しかし、会社の宴会などの最後には今でもときどき「万歳！」が聞かれます。ジョン・ウェインの映画ファンの中には「万歳」という言葉の意味を勘違いしている人もいるか

present is about to fix bayonets, as some aficionados of John Wayne films may mistakenly believe. It literally means "10,000 years" and toasts the emperor's long life (or, indeed, the longevity and prosperity of other, non-Emperor related pursuits).

Part 2

The use of *kampai* and *banzai* as drinking toasts appears to be a relatively new phenomenon. Wherever there are drinkers there is always going to be someone who thinks a few words goes well with the first glass, but it was the arrival of Western diplomats in the Meiji period (1868–1912) that formalized Japanese toasts. The foreigners were forever toasting their kings and presidents and so, not to be outdone, the Japanese representatives started shouting *banzai* to the emperor. Later, in the 1910s and 1920s, *kampai!* (from the Chinese exhortation *kampei!*, "Drain your glass") began to establish itself as a less emperor-centric alternative to *banzai!*

Part 3

Pouring for others

It is a customary when drinking in a group in Japan to pour other people's drinks, and it is polite to wait for others in the group to pour yours. This may sound overly formal to the uninitiated but can be a great way for foreigners having difficulty with the language to interact and make friends. I have known this custom to be used to strike up conversations with people in adjoining groups too.

もしれませんが、「万歳」は全員が銃剣を構える合図ではありません。「万歳」は文字通り「一万年」を意味し、天皇の長寿を祝う乾杯の言葉です。(また、天皇以外の人々の長寿や繁栄を祝うのにも使われます。)

Part 2

「乾杯」や「万歳」を飲み会で使うのは比較的新しい習慣のようです。どこにでも最初の一杯に言葉を添えたいと思う人がいるものですが、日本での乾杯の習慣が正式に始まったのは、明治時代 (1868年-1912年) に西洋の外交官たちがやってきたときのことです。外国人たちはいつも自分たちの王様や大統領に向けて乾杯していましたが、それに負けじと日本の代表者たちも天皇に向けて「万歳！」を叫びはじめたのです。その後、1910年代から1920年代にかけて、「乾杯！」(中国語の「乾杯！」が由来で「グラスを空にする」という意味) が、天皇を中心としない乾杯の言葉として定着していきました。

Part 3

お酌

日本では、グループで飲むときに他の人に飲み物を注いであげるのが習慣です。そして、自分の飲み物を他の人に注いでもらうのを待つのが礼儀です。この習慣ははじめての人には少し形式的に思えるかもしれませんが、外国人が言葉の壁を乗り越えて人と仲良くなるための良い方法です。隣のグループの人たちと話しを始めるきっかけとしても使われることがあります。

Part 4

If you want to be really polite, pour while holding the bottle in two hands and hold your glass in two hands when receiving. If possible, try to accept drinks offered by people in the group who have not poured for you and swiftly pick up the bottle and pour for them (in many cases, people are pouring because they want their glass refilled). None of these customs should be taken as being set in stone.

Part 5

Plenty of people pour their own drinks in group situations. In general, it is not the done thing to drink directly from bottles, although there are young people's hangouts where this is de rigueur. Where a glass is provided, it is best to use it.

Part 6

The importance of being frank

Many Japanese people look upon office parties as a sort of safety valve. The theory goes that lowly workers should be able to talk honestly to their bosses about feelings they would not normally be able to express. Everybody is supposed to relax, act and talk freely and forget about any indiscretions in the morning. But tread carefully! There may be more politics going on than you think.

Part 4

礼儀正しくしたい場合は、ボトルを両手で持って注ぎ、注いでもらうときは自分のグラスを両手で持ちます。また、できれば、まだ注いでもらっていない人に注いでもらい、その後すぐにその人にお返しに注いであげると良いでしょう（たいてい人は自分のグラスを満たしてもらいたいから人のグラスに注いでいるのです）。これらのお酌の習慣はどれも厳格なものではありません。

Part 5

グループで飲むときに自分で注ぐ人もたくさんいます。一般的には、ボトルから直接飲むのは普通ではありませんが、若者が集まる場所ではそれが普通であることもあります。グラスが用意されている場合は、それを使うのが良いでしょう。

Part 6

本音で話すことの重要性

多くの日本人にとって職場の飲み会は一種の安全弁のようなものです。理論的には部下が普段は言えないことを上司に正直に話せる場とされています。皆がリラックスして自由に話し、次の日にはその失言を忘れるということになっています。しかし、注意はいつも必要です！実際には飲み会では思っている以上に複雑な駆け引きがあるかもしれません。

Part 7

In 1323, courtiers acting under the auspices of the Emperor Go-Daigo started organizing *bureikō* parties. *Bureikō* meant "putting aside rank" and is still the term used for the frankness encouraged at office gatherings. At Go-Daigo's original *bureikō* parties, humble warriors and priests were allowed to mix with favored members of the court. Sake and food were consumed in great quantities. Everybody let down their hair, dressed simply and was prompted to speak honestly about their frustrations, politics and hopes for the future. These curious events were not taken seriously by the Kamakura shogunate, the warrior government which had a stranglehold over the imperial state at the time, but were the first steps in building support for Go-Daigo's long and eventually successful campaign to smash the shogunate.

Vocabulary and Expressions

PART 1

乾杯！ **Kampai!** Cheers!

飲み会 **nomikai** drinking party

たいてい **taitei** usually

始まる **hajimaru** to begin (intransitive verb)

大きな声で **ōkina koe de** in a loud voice

皆 **mina** everyone

そろって **sorotte** together

叫ぶ **sakebu** to shout; to scream

…まで **... made** until ...

飲む **nomu** to drink

…はじめる **...hajimeru** to begin to ... (following a verb in the stem form)

礼儀 **reigi** manners

もう一つ **mō hitotsu** one more

Part 7

　1323年、後醍醐天皇の側近たちが「無礼講」と呼ばれる宴会を開きはじめました。無礼講とは「身分を超えた交流」を意味し、職場の集まりで本音を話すことを促す言葉として今でも使われています。後醍醐天皇の最初の無礼講では、身分の低い武士や僧侶が宮廷の選ばれた人物と交流することが許されていました。大量の酒と食べ物が出され、皆がくつろぎ、簡素な服装で不満や、政治や、未来への希望などについて正直に話すことが奨励されました。この変わった宴会は、当時皇室を抑え込んでいた武士政権である鎌倉幕府には真剣に受け止められていませんでした。しかし、後醍醐天皇は長い戦いの末やがて幕府を倒すのに成功しますが、この無礼講はその支持を築くのに不可欠だったのです。

言葉 **kotoba** word

万歳！ **Banzai!** Banzai!; Hurray!

昔　**mukashi** in the past

…ほど…ない **... hodo ... nai** not as ... as ...

人気 **ninki** popularity

会社 **kaisha** company

宴会 **enkai** banquet; party

…など **... nado** such as ...; etc.

最後 **saigo** last; final

今 **ima** now

…でも **...demo** even ...

ときどき **tokidoki** sometimes

聞かれる **kikareru** to be heard (passive form of 聞く **kiku** to hear; to listen)

…という **...to iu** called ...

映画 **eiga** movie

Nihon no nomi bunka

意味 **imi** meaning

勘違いする **kanchigai suru** to misunderstand

…かもしれない **... kamo shirenai** might ...

…が **...ga** but

全員 **zen'in** all members

銃剣 **jūken** bayonet

構える **kamaeru** to prepare

合図 **aizu** signal

文字通り **mojidōri** literally

一万年 **ichiman-nen** ten thousand years

天皇 **tennō** emperor

長寿 **chōju** longevity

祝う **iwau** to celebrate

…以外 **... igai** except for ...

人々 **hitobito** people

繁栄 **han'ei** prosperity

使われる **tsukawareru** to be used (passive form of 使う **tsukau** to use)

PART 2

比較的 **hikakuteki** comparatively

新しい **atarashii** new

習慣 **shūkan** custom

…のようだ **...no yō da** appears to be ... (following a noun)

どこにでも **doko ni demo** anywhere

最初の **saisho no** first

一杯 **ippai** one glass

添える **soeru** to add; to accompany

…たい **...tai** to want to ... (following a verb in the stem form)

思う **omou** to think

正式に **seishiki ni** formally

明治時代 **Meiji jidai** the Meiji era

西洋 **seiyō** the West

外交官 **gaikōkan** diplomat

…たち **...tachi** plural suffix for people and animals

やってくる **yatte kuru** to come; to arrive

とき **toki** time

外国人 **gaikokujin** foreigner

いつも **itsumo** always

自分 **jibun** oneself

王様 **ōsama** king

大統領 **daitōryō** president

…に向けて **... ni mukete** toward ...; for ...

負けじと **makeji to** not to be outdone

代表者 **daihyō-sha** representative

その後 **sonogo** after that

…年代 **...nendai** ... decade

中国語 **Chūgokugo** Chinese language

由来 **yurai** origin

空にする **kara ni suru** to empty

中心 **chūshin** center; core

…として **...toshite** as ...

定着する **teichaku suru** to become established

(…て) いく **(...te) iku** to continue to ...; to go on ... (following a verb in the **te**-form)

PART 3

お酌 **o-shaku** pouring sake into others' glasses

他の… **hoka no ...** other ...

飲み物 **nomimono** drink

注ぐ **tsugu** to pour

(…て) あげる **(...te) ageru** to do (something) for someone (following a verb in the **te**-form)

(…て) もらう **(...te) morau** to receive (someone's action) (following a verb in the **te**-form)

待つ **matsu** to wait

少し **sukoshi** a little

形式的 **keishikiteki** formal

思える **omoeru** to seem; to appear

…かもしれない **... kamo shirenai** might ...

外国人 **gaikokujin** foreigner

壁 **kabe** wall

乗り越える **norikoeru** to overcome

仲良くなる **nakayoku naru** to become close

…ため **... tame** for the purpose of ...

良い **yoi** good

方法 **hōhō** method; way

隣の **tonari no** next door

話し **hanashi** talk; conversation

始める **hajimeru** to start (transitive verb)

きっかけ **kikkake** trigger; opportunity

…ことがある **... koto ga aru** there are times when ... (following a verb in the plain non-past form)

Nihon no nomi bunka

PART 4

礼儀正しくする **reigitadashiku suru** to behave appropriately politely

…たい **…tai** want to … (following a verb in the stem form)

場合 **baai** situation; case

両手で **ryōte de** with both hands

持つ **motsu** to hold

できれば **dekireba** if possible

まだ **mada** still; yet

その後 **sono ato** after that

お返しに **okaeshi ni** in return

満たす **mitasu** to fill

どれも（…ない）**doremo (…nai)** none of them

厳格な **genkaku na** strict; serious

PART 5

一般的に **ippanteki ni** generally; typically

直接 **chokusetsu** directly

普通 **futsū** normal; ordinary

若者 **wakamono** young people

集まる **atsumaru** to gather (intransitive verb)

場所 **basho** place; location

用意する **yōi suru** to prepare

PART 6

本音 **honne** true feelings; real intention

重要性 **jūyōsei** importance

多くの **ōku no** many; a lot of

職場 **shokuba** workplace

一種の… **isshu no …** a kind of …

安全弁 **anzenben** safety valve

…のような **…no yō na** like …; similar to …

理論的には **rironteki ni wa** theoretically

部下 **buka** subordinate

普段 **fudan** usually; ordinarily

言えない **ienai** cannot say (negative potential form of 言う **iu** to say)

上司 **jōshi** boss; superior

正直に **shōjiki ni** honestly; truthfully

場 **ba** place

自由に **jiyū ni** freely

次の日 **tsugi no hi** the next day

失言 **shitsugen** slip of the tongue

忘れる **wasureru** to forget

…ことになっている **… koto ni natte iru** it is supposed to …

注意 chūi caution; attention

必要 hitsuyō necessary

実際には jissai ni wa in reality; actually

…以上に ...ijō ni more than ...

複雑な fukuzatsu na complicated; complex

駆け引き kakehiki negotiation; diplomacy

PART 7

側近 sokkin close associate

呼ばれる yobareru to be called (passive form of 呼ぶ yobu to call)

開く hiraku to open

身分 mibun social status

超える koeru to surpass

交流 kōryū interaction

促す unagasu to encourage; to promote

最初の… saisho no ... the first ...

身分の低い mibun no hikui of low social status

武士 bushi warrior; samurai

僧侶 sōryo monk

宮廷 kyūtei court; palace

選ばれた erabareta chosen; selected

人物 jinbutsu person; figure

許される yurusareru to be allowed; to be permitted

大量 tairyō large quantity; a great amount

酒 sake alcohol

食べ物 tabemono food

出される dasareru to be brought out (passive form of 出す dasu to bring out)

くつろぐ kutsurogu to relax

簡素な kanso na simple; plain

服装 fukusō clothing; attire

不満 fuman frustration; complaint

政治 seiji politics

未来 mirai future

希望 kibō hope; wish

…について ... ni tsuite about ...

奨励 shōrei encouragement

変わった kawatta unusual; different

当時 tōji at that time

皇室 kōshitsu imperial family

抑え込む osaekomu to suppress

武士政権 bushi seiken samurai government; warrior regime

鎌倉 **Kamakura** Kamakura (city)
幕府 **bakufu** shogunate
真剣 **shinken** seriousness; earnestness
受け止める **uketomeru** to take seriously; to accept
長い **nagai** long
戦い **tatakai** battle; fight

…の末 **...no sue** at the end of …
やがて **yagate** eventually
倒す **taosu** to overthrow
成功 **seikō** success
支持 **shiji** support
築く **kizuku** to build; to establish
不可欠 **fukaketsu** indispensable; essential

Comprehension and Language

Select the most appropriate answer in the parentheses or fill in the gap.

1. 日本の飲み会では皆で「乾杯！」と叫ぶまでは飲みはじめ（る・ない）のが礼儀だ。

2. 会社の宴会などの最後にはときどき＿＿＿＿＿＿という言葉が使われることもある。

3. これらの言葉は（明治・鎌倉）時代に使われはじめた。

4. 日本では他の人のグラスに飲み物を注いで（あげる・もらう）。

5. それから、他の人に自分のグラスに飲み物を注いで（あげる・もらう）。

6. ボトルやグラスは両手（で・を）持つのが礼儀だ。

7. 無礼講は一種の安全弁の（ような・らしい）ものだ。

8. 無礼講では部下が＿＿＿＿に普段言えないことを話せる。
9. 無礼講は後醍醐天皇が幕府打倒を倒すための＿＿＿＿を築くのに不可欠だった。

Discussion Points

1. What are the customs surrounding drinking in your culture? How do they differ from those in Japan?
2. What significance does the story of the origin of *bureikō* hold? What can we learn from it?
3. Do you think adopting *bureikō* practices would benefit companies and organizations in your country? Why or why not?

Dating Opportunities

Japan has some unique dating and matchmaking activities, which have become popular ways to find a future husband, wife or significant other.

> **Key words**
> 出会う **deau** to meet; to encounter
> 合コン **gō-kon** group blind date
> 街コン **machi-kon** town-wide matchmaking event

Part 1

Sayuri Nagano first met her husband at a *gokon*, a group blind date. The gokon is a type of social event that started in the 1970s, where college students organized heteronormative gatherings, bringing together one group of men and one group of women. Typically, a gokon involves an equal number of participants from each group, for example, three men and three women. The group meets at a restaurant or bar and engages in natural and casual conversation over dinner or drinks. You may find someone you like within a few hours, and exchange phone numbers. The Japanese TV romcom *Yamato Nadeshiko* (2000) depicts gokon well.

出会いのチャンス
Deai no chansu

Part 1

長野佐友里さんが最初にご主人と出会ったのは「合コン」というグループデートだった。合コンは男女が集まって飲食を楽しむ場で1970年代ごろに始まった。通常、合コンには同数の男性と女性が参加する。たとえば、三人の男性と三人の女性が集まり、レストランやバーで自然に会話を楽しむ。数時間で気が合った人が見つかることもあり、同日に連絡先を交換する可能性もある。日本のテレビドラマ『やまとなでしこ』(2000年)を見ると合コンがどんなものかよくわかるだろう。

Part 2

"I went to a lot of gokon, like five times a week, or at least three times a week!" says Sayuri. "I kept that up for about a year."

According to Sayuri, the probability of finding a future lifetime partner through one gokon is not high. Therefore, she recommends not to have high expectations for each gokon, but rather to enjoy socializing and take the opportunity to learn more about others and more about yourself.

Part 3

For those frustrated by the slow pace of meeting only a few new people at each gokon, a *machikon*—a large-scale gokon organized by private matchmaking companies—might be more appealing. Machikon events can involve over one hundred participants and take place in a wide variety of venues, such as restaurants, pubs or karaoke rooms, all within walking distance in a particular town or *machi*.

Part 4

Yokkich, a YouTube personality, participated in a machikon in his suburban town. The participation fee was ¥8,300 (about US$60) for men and ¥1,000 (about US$7) for women. Yokkich paid the fee and visited multiple designated venues, enjoying food and drinks while having conversations with other participants in a rotating group setting. Toward the end, all participants were asked to list the top three people of the opposite sex they'd like to meet again, and the match results were announced shortly afterward. Although his first choice did not select him, his second and third choices did. Yokkich reflected that it was a fun day and that he enjoyed the overall experience.

Part 2

　「とにかくたくさん合コンをしたんですね。週5とか少なくても週3くらいで！それを1年くらいやっていました。」と長野さんは言う。長野さんによると、合コンで将来のパートナーを見つける確率はあまり高くない。そのため、合コンにはあまり期待しすぎないで、社交を楽しんだり、他の人や自分自身を知ったりする良い機会だと考えるべきだということだ。

Part 3

　もし、合コンで出会える人の数が少なすぎると感じるなら、街コンに参加してみるのも良いかもしれない。街コンは大規模な合コンのようなもので、婚活支援企業などが主催し、100人以上の参加者が集まることが多い。レストランや居酒屋、カラオケなど、街の中で歩いて行ける数か所で行われる。

Part 4

　YouTubeで活動するYokkichさんは自分の住んでいる郊外で行われた街コンに参加した。男性の参加費は8,300円（約60ドル）、女性の参加費は1,000円（約7ドル）だった。Yokkichさんは、8,300円払い、指定された複数の場所を次々に訪れ、食事や飲み物を楽しみながら、ローテーション形式で他の参加者と会話をした。イベントの最後には再び会いたい異性を三人選ばせられた。その結果はすぐに発表され、Yokkichさんは自分の第1希望の人には選ばれなかったが、第2希望と第3希望の人には選ばれた。全体的に楽しい一日だったと感じたそうだ。

Part 5

For those who haven't found a romantic partner through school or work, gokon and machikon can be fun ways to expand your chances of meeting someone. Just be mindful not to overindulge in alcohol!

Vocabulary and Expressions

PART 1

最初に **saisho ni** first; for the first time

ご主人 **go-shujin** husband (honorific)

出会う **deau** to meet; to encounter

男女 **danjo** men and women

集まる **atsumaru** to gather (intransitive verb)

飲食 **inshoku** eating and drinking

楽しむ **tanoshimu** to enjoy

場 **ba** place; occasion

…年代 **...nendai** ... decade (1970年代 the 1970s)

…ごろ **...goro** around ... (time); ...about (time)

始まる **hajimaru** to begin

通常 **tsūjō** usually; commonly

同数 **dōsū** equal number

男性 **dansei** man; male

女性 **josei** woman; female

参加する **sanka suru** to participate

たとえば **tatoeba** for example

自然に **shizen ni** naturally

会話 **kaiwa** conversation

数時間 **sūjikan** several hours

気が合う **ki ga au** to get along

見つかる **mitsukaru** to be found

同日に **dōjitsu ni** on the same day

連絡先 **renraku saki** contact information

交換する **kōkan suru** to exchange

可能性 **kanōsei** possibility

わかる **wakaru** to understand

…だろう **...darō** It is probably the case that ...

Part 5

　学校や職場で恋人が見つからなかった人にとって合コンや街コンは出会いのチャンスを広げる楽しい方法かもしれない。ただし、お酒の飲みすぎには注意が必要だろう。

PART 2

とにかく **tonikaku** anyway; in any case

週 **shū** week

少なくても **sukunakute mo** at least

…くらい **...kurai** approximately …

言う **iu** to say

将来 **shōrai** future

見つける **mitsukeru** to find

確率 **kakuritsu** probability

高い **takai** high

そのため **sonotame** for that reason

期待する **kitai suru** to expect

…すぎる **...sugiru** to do/be … too much (following a verb or an adjective in the stem form)

(…た)り **(... ta)ri** to do … etc. (following a verb in the **ta**-form)

他の人 **hoka no hito** other people

自分自身 **jibun jishin** oneself

知る **shiru** to get to know

良い **yoi** good

機会 **kikai** opportunity

考える **kangaeru** to think

…べきだ **...beki da** should …; ought to … (following a verb in the plain affirmative form)

…ということだ **...to iu koto da** to be the case that …

PART 3

もし… **moshi ...** if …

出会える **deaeru** to be able to encounter (potential form of 出会う **deau** to encounter)

数 **kazu** number

少ない **sukunai** few; scarce

感じる **kanjiru** to feel

…なら **...nara** if …

Deai no chansu 159

参加する sanka suru to participate

(…て) みる (...te) miru to try ...ing (following a verb in the te-form)

…かもしれない ... kamo shirenai it is possible that ...

大規模な daikibo na large-scale

…のような ...no yō na like ...; such as ...

婚活支援 konkatsu shien marriage support

企業 kigyō company

…など ...nado etc.; and so on

主催する shusai suru to host; to organize

…以上 ...ijō ... or more

…者 ...sha (suffix) person associated with a particular role

多い ōi many; numerous

居酒屋 izakaya izakaya (Japanese pub)

街 machi town; city

歩く aruku to walk

行ける ikeru to be able to go (potential form of 行く iku to go)

数か所 sūkasho several places

行われる okonawareru to be held (passive form of 行う okonau to hold; to perform)

PART 4

活動する katsudō suru to engage in activity

自分 jibun oneself

住む sumu to live

郊外 kōgai suburb

…費 ...hi cost of ...

…円 ...en ... yen

約… yaku ... approximately ...

払う harau to pay

指定 shitei designation; specification

複数の… fukusū no ... multiple ...

場所 basho place; location

次々に tsugitsugi ni one after another

訪れる otozureru to visit

形式 keishiki form; format

最後に saigo ni at the end

再び futatabi again

会う au to meet

…たい ... tai to want to ... (following a verb in the stem form)

異性 isei opposite sex

選^{えら}ばせられる **erabaserareru** to be made to choose (causative passive form of 選^{えら}ぶ **erabu** to choose)

結果^{けっか} **kekka** result

発表^{はっぴょう} **happyō** announcement

第^{だい}1希望^{きぼう} **daiichi kibō** first choice

選^{えら}ばれる **erabareru** to be chosen (passive form of 選^{えら}ぶ **erabu** to choose)

⋯が **...ga** but

全体的^{ぜんたいてき}に **zentaiteki ni** overall; generally

一日^{いちにち} **ichinichi** one day; a whole day

感^{かん}じる **kanjiru** to feel

⋯そうだ **...sō da** They say that ... (hearsay) (following a verb or adjective in the plain form)

PART 5

学校^{がっこう} **gakkō** school

職場^{しょくば} **shokuba** workplace

恋人^{こいびと} **koibito** lover; partner

⋯にとって **... ni totte** for ...; from the perspective of ...

広^{ひろ}げる **hirogeru** to expand; to broaden

方法^{ほうほう} **hōhō** method; way

ただし **tadashi** however; but

お酒^{さけ} **osake** alcohol

飲^のみすぎ **nomisugi** drinking too much

注意^{ちゅうい} **chūi** caution; attention

必要^{ひつよう} **hitsuyō** necessity; need

⋯だろう **...darō** I guess ...

Deai no chansu

Comprehension and Language

Select the most appropriate answer in the parentheses or fill in the gap.

1. 合コンは1970年代ごろ（に・で）始まった。
2. 合コンでは同数の男女が集まり、食事、飲み物、会話など（を・に）楽しむ。
3. 合コンは社交を楽しんだり、他の人や自分自身を知ったり（する・しない）良い機会だとも考えられる。
4. その一方、街コンは大規模な＿＿＿＿＿＿＿＿のようなものだ。
5. 街コンは婚活支援企業などが主催し、100人以上の参加者が（集まる・集める）ことが多い。
6. 街コンでは街の中の指定された複数の＿＿＿＿＿＿を次々に訪れ、食事や飲み物を楽しみながら、他の参加者と会話ができる。
7. 学校や職場で恋人が見つからなかった人（に・で）とって合コンや街コンは出会いのチャンスを広げる楽しい方法かもしれない。

Discussion Points

1. Do you think it's harder to meet new people today compared to fifty years ago in your country? Why or why not?
2. How do gokon and machikon differ? What are the main advantages and disadvantages of each? Would you have a preference?
3. In comparison to dating apps, what are the benefits and drawbacks of gokon and machikon? Which do you think is more effective for meeting a romantic partner?

Why I Love Japan Even More since the Earthquake

by David McNeill

Tokyo-based journalist David McNeill gives a firsthand account of his experience of the Tohoku earthquake in 2011 and its aftermath.

Key words

地震 **jishin** earthquake

放射能 **hōshanō** radiation

気質 **kishitsu** temperament; disposition

Part 1

In March 2011, a week after the Tohoku earthquake, tsunami and consequent meltdown of the Fukushima Daiichi Nuclear Power Plant, when many of my spooked friends had already decamped west, south or abroad, I urged my pregnant partner Nanako to leave Tokyo for the apparent safety of western Japan. She wasn't happy and for good reason: I was staying behind, her parents were in Tokyo and she knew nobody in Osaka. Two days before, my sister and boyfriend had cut short a hol-

震災後に日本がさらに好きになった理由
Shinsai go ni nihon ga sara ni suki ni natta riyū

デイビッド・マックニール

Part 1

2011年3月11日、東北で地震と津波が起きた。一週間後、福島第一原発がメルトダウンした。私の友人の多くは恐れをいだき、すでに西へと、南へと、または国外へと向かってしまっていた。そのとき、私は妊娠中のパートナー、菜奈子に安全な関西に避難するよう勧めた。菜奈子は不満だったが、それはもっともだった。私は東京に残り、菜奈子の両親も東京に在住、そして大阪には知り合いがいなかったからだ。二日前、私の妹と妹の

iday in Japan and flown to Hong Kong after a painful haranguing from my mother in Ireland.

Part 2

Before Nanako and I left for Shinagawa Station there was another strong earthquake, a report on the radio about potentially catastrophic radiation from the Fukushima plant and a warning by the Irish Embassy in Tokyo that pregnant women should avoid the capital.

Part 3

Exhausted and emotional after Nanako's tearful departure, I headed for a coffee shop in the station where four perfectly turned-out waitresses serenaded my entry with a singsong *"Irrashaimase!"* and fussed over my order with typically attentive service.

Part 4

"Take your time," said a beaming young woman as she passed me my coffee. At which point I started crying.

彼氏は、母親から厳しく責め立てられ、日本での旅行を切り上げ、香港へ飛んでいた。

Part 2

菜奈子と私が品川駅に向かう前に、また大きな地震があり、ラジオでは福島原発からの放射能が危険だという報道が流れ、東京のアイルランド大使館からは、妊婦は東京を避けるようにとの警告があった。

Part 3

菜奈子が涙ながらに出発した後、肉体的にも感情的にも疲れ果てたまま駅のカフェに行った。そこでは、四人の店員が「いらっしゃいませ！」と明るく私を迎えてくれ、私の注文を丁寧に取ってくれた。

Part 4

「ごゆっくりどうぞ」コーヒーを手渡してくれた若い女性は、笑顔で言ってくれた。その瞬間、私は涙がこぼれた。

Part 5

Admirable ability

I wrote something later that day for *The Irish Times*, pondering this admirable and mysterious ability of many Japanese people to function normally as the scenery collapses around them. How black-suited salarymen stayed at their posts, housewives calmly queued for water and fuel, and waitresses still acted as though the most important thing in the world was my ¥280 [$1.80] order.

Part 6

Some say that these people are just falling back on routine because they don't know any better.

Part 7

"Robots," said one of my friends disparagingly, after I told him how a video store clerk kept calling during the week to remind me to return an overdue DVD.

Part 8

But I don't agree. Those waitresses are human beings with families, who worry about radiation too. I like to think they stay focused because to not do so is to let down others, and that invites chaos.

Part 5
敬服すべき能力
　その日、私は『アイリッシュ・タイムズ』に向けて執筆した。思いを巡らせていたのは、周囲の状況が崩れ去っていく中でも、たくさんの日本人が平然と日常生活を送るこの敬服すべき不思議な能力だった。黒いスーツを着たサラリーマンは自分の任務を離れず、主婦は水や燃料のために落ち着いて列に並び、ウェイトレスは私の280円の注文がまるで世界で一番大事なことのように扱ってくれていた。

Part 6
　「この人達は他にすべをしらないから、平常にしがみついているだけだ」と言った者もいた。

Part 7
　「ロボットみたいだ」と友人の一人も言った。私が返し忘れていたDVDを返却するようビデオ店の店員から何度も電話があったことを話したときだった。

Part 8
　でも、私にはそうは思えない。あのウェイトレスたちも人間だ。だから、家族もいるし放射能を心配しているはずだ。彼らがちゃんと仕事をこなしつづけるのは、そうしないと他の人たちをがっかりさせ、混乱を招くからだと私は思いたい。

Part 9

Uprooted communities

I traveled north twice to visit refugee centers in Tohoku, the epicenter of the earthquake, and was often moved by what I saw. In Rikuzen-Takata, the muddy deluge of March 11 had torn the town from its roots, leaving a gaping wound of smashed cars, pulverized wooden houses and twisted metal girders.

Part 10

Car navigation systems still directed visitors to the post office and the local government building, which were no longer there. But in the makeshift refugee center, you could clearly see why this community would bounce back.

Part 11

Local people in a school gym had organized themselves into temporary neighborhoods tagged with signs identifying the now destroyed district to which they belonged—an infinitely more resilient structure than the flimsy wooden houses washed into the sea.

Part 12

Food, water and baths were carefully and seamlessly rationed. Housewives, teachers and firemen stepped into leadership roles. Older children told younger children what to do during aftershocks. There were no fights about who got what.

Part 9

根こそぎにされたコミュニティ

　私は地震の震源地である東北の避難所を二回訪れた。そこで見た光景にはやはり心を打たれた。陸前高田では、3月11日の泥水で町を根こそぎにされていて、そこにはぽっかりと大きく開いた傷跡があり、壊れた車、粉々になった木造家屋、そして曲がった金属の骨組みなどがその傷跡を覆っていた。

Part 10

　カーナビはまだ郵便局や役所に案内するが、それらはもう存在していない。しかし、仮設の避難所では、このコミュニティーが立ち直るだろうという確実なきざしがはっきりと見えた。

Part 11

　学校の体育館では、地元の人たちは今は破壊されて跡形もなく消えてしまった自分達の地区の名前を書いたサインを掲げて、しっかりしたコミュニティーをつくりあげていた。これは、海に流された木造家屋よりもはるかに強固なコミュニティーの形だった。

Part 12

　食料、水、そして風呂の時間は注意深く分けられ、無駄がないように分配されていた。主婦、教師、消防士がリーダーシップを取り、年長の子供たちは余震のときに何をすべきかを年少の子供たちに教えていた。誰が何をもらったかどうかなどと言って喧嘩することはなかった。

Part 13

Outside the town, a hot springs resort had been converted into another temporary shelter, housing old people and families.

Part 14

Every day, hundreds of people were bussed in for a bath, a vital psychological boost. Everyone got thirty minutes, roughly once a fortnight.

Part 15

Anyone who knows the importance of baths in this country will appreciate how much endurance it takes for people to restrict themselves to that meager ration. Yet nobody, not even the people who ran the resort, broke the rule. "If I did that, it would get around and the system would break down," one worker told me.

Part 13

町の外では、温泉リゾートが追加の仮設避難所に改装され、高齢者とその家族をそこに住まわせていた。

Part 14

毎日、何百人もの人々がバスでお風呂に運ばれ、心理的に大きな助けになった。みんな30分間、だいたい二週間に一度だけお風呂に入ることができた。

Part 15

この国でお風呂がどれだけ大切か知っている人なら、それを我慢するのがどれほど大変か理解できるだろう。それでも、誰一人として、リゾートのスタッフでさえ、このルールを破る人はいなかった。「もし私がルールを破ったら、すぐに噂が広まって、システムが崩壊してしまう」と、あるスタッフが私に言った。

Part 16

In it together

Above all, what will stay with me after these communities are rebuilt, the Fukushima plant encased in a concrete coffin, and the iodine, cesium and plutonium have stopped seeping from its bowels, is the way Japanese people carried themselves during this crisis.

Part 17

I'm thinking now of the smiles I saw around Iwate, of the many old people and children in the prefecture who shoved food into my hands and told me to keep going.

Part 18

I think these qualities are social, not genetic, built up over generations, and possibly stronger in the northeast, where life has traditionally been harsher. But whatever the reason, it works. And I'm staying.

Vocabulary and Expressions

PART 1

震災後 **shinsai-go** after the earthquake disaster

2011年3月11日 **2011-nen 3-gatsu 11-nichi** March 11, 2011

東北 **Tōhoku** Tohoku (northeastern region of Japan)

地震 **jishin** earthquake

津波 **tsunami** tsunami

起きる **okiru** to occur

一週間後 **isshūkan-go** one week later

福島第一原発 **Fukushima Daiichi Genpatsu** Fukushima Daiichi Nuclear Power Plant

友人 **yūjin** friend

Part 16

一緒にそこにいた

これらのコミュニティーが再建され、福島原発がコンクリートの棺に覆われ、ヨウ素、セシウム、プルトニウムの流出が止まった後に、私の心に残るのは、なによりもこの危機の中を日本の人々が一緒にどう立ち振る舞ったかということだろう。

Part 17

今、私は岩手で見た笑顔や、食べ物を私の手に押し込んで「がんばって」と言ってくれたたくさんの老人や子供たちのことを思い出している。

Part 18

これらの素晴らしい気質は、遺伝子によるものではなく、長い年月をかけて育まれた社会的なものであり、特に昔から生活が厳しかった東北で顕著に見られるものだと思う。しかし、理由が何であれ、それは確かに意味を持つ。だから、私はここに残る。

多く **ōku** many

恐れをいだき **osore o idaki** filled with fear

すでに **sude ni** already

西 **nishi** west

南 **minami** south

国外 **kokugai** overseas; abroad

向かう **mukau** to head toward

(…て) しまう **(... te) shimau** to end up ...ing (following **te**-form verb)

妊娠中 **ninshinchū** during pregnancy

安全な **anzen na** safe

関西 **Kansai** Kansai (region in western Japan)

避難する hinan suru to evacuate

勧める susumeru to recommend; to advise

不満 fuman dissatisfaction; discontent

もっともだ mottomo da it makes sense; it's reasonable

残る nokoru to remain

両親 ryōshin parents

在住 zaijū residence; living in

知り合い shiriai acquaintance

…から だ …kara da it is because …

二日前 futsuka mae two days before

彼氏 kareshi boyfriend

母親 hahaoya mother

厳しく kibishiku strictly; harshly

責め立てられる semetaterareru to be harshly criticized (passive form of 責め立てる semetateru to blame)

旅行 ryokō trip; travel

切り上げる kiriageru to cut short

香港 Honkon Hong Kong

飛ぶ tobu to fly

PART 2

…前に …mae ni before …

危険だ kiken da dangerous

報道 hōdō news report

流れる nagareru to be broadcast; to flow

大使館 taishikan embassy

妊婦 ninpu pregnant woman

避ける sakeru to avoid

警告 keikoku warning

PART 3

涙ながらに namida nagara ni with tears; tearfully

出発する shuppatsu suru to depart

…後 …ato after … (following a verb in the **ta**-form)

肉体的に nikutaiteki ni physically

感情的に kanjōteki ni emotionally

疲れ果てる tsukare-hateru to be completely exhausted

(…た) まま (… ta) mama as one keeps …ing (following a verb in the **ta**-form)

駅 eki station

四人 yonin four people

店員 ten'in store clerk

明るく akaruku cheerfully; brightly

迎える mukaeru to welcome

(…て) くれる (...te) kureru to do (something for me) (following a verb in the te-form)

注文 chūmon order

丁寧に teinei ni politely; carefully

PART 4

手渡す tewatasu to hand over

若い wakai young

女性 josei woman

笑顔で egao de with a smile

その瞬間 sono shunkan that moment

涙 namida tears

こぼれる koboreru to spill; to overflow

PART 5

敬服すべき keifuku subeki admirable; worthy of respect

能力 nōryoku ability

…に向けて ... ni mukete toward ...; aimed at ...

執筆する shippitsu suru to write

思いを巡らせる omoi o meguraseru to reflect; to ponder

周囲 shūi surroundings; environment

状況 jōkyō situation

崩れ去る kuzuresaru to collapse completely; to fall apart

平然と heizen to calmly; without flinching

日常生活を送る nichijō seikatsu o okuru to live one's daily life

不思議な fushigi na mysterious; strange

黒い kuroi black

着る kiru to wear; to put on

自分 jibun oneself

任務 ninmu duty; task

離れず hanarezu without leaving; staying close

主婦 shufu housewife

水 mizu water

燃料 nenryō fuel

…のために ... no tame ni for the purpose of ...

落ち着いて ochitsuite calmly; composedly

列に並ぶ **retsu ni narabu** to line up; to stand in line

世界で一番 **sekai de ichiban** the most important in the world

大事な **daiji na** important; crucial

扱う **atsukau** to handle; to deal with

PART 6

他にすべをしらない **hoka ni sube o shiranai** not knowing any other way

日常 **nichijō** daily

しがみつく **shigamitsuku** to cling to

…だけだ **... dake da** it is only …; just …

者 **mono** person

PART 7

…みたいだ **...mitai da** to look like … (following a noun)

友人 **yūjin** friend

返し忘れる **kaeshi-wasureru** to forget to return

返却する **henkyaku suru** to return (an item)

ビデオ店 **bideo ten** video store

店員 **ten'in** store clerk

何度も **nando mo** many times

電話 **denwa** phone

話す **hanasu** to talk

PART 8

思える **omoeru** to seem; to appear (potential form of 思う **omou** to think)

人間 **ningen** human

家族 **kazoku** family

心配する **shinpai suru** to worry

…はずだ **...hazu da** should …; ought to …

彼ら **karera** they; them

仕事 **shigoto** work; job

こなす **konasu** to manage; to handle

…つづける **...tsuzukeru** to continue to … (following a verb in the stem form)

そうしないと **sō shinai to** if not; otherwise

他の人たち **hoka no hitotachi** other people

がっかりさせる **gakkari saseru** to disappoint (someone)

混乱 **konran** chaos; confusion

招く **maneku** to invite; to cause

…たい **...tai** to want to … (following a verb in the stem form)

PART 9

根こそぎにされる nekosogi ni sareru to be uprooted

震源地 shingenchi epicenter

避難所 hinanjo evacuation center; shelter

二回 ni-kai twice

訪れる otozureru to visit

見る miru to see

光景 kōkei scene; sight

やはり yahari as expected; indeed

心を打たれる kokoro o utareru to be deeply moved; to be struck emotionally

泥水 deisui muddy water

町 machi town

ぽっかりと pokkari to gaping; wide open (mimetic)

開く hiraku to open

傷跡 kizuato scar; wound

壊れる kowareru to break; to be destroyed

車 kuruma car

粉々になる konagona ni naru to be shattered into pieces

木造家屋 mokuzō kaoku wooden house

曲がる magaru to bend

金属 kinzoku metal

骨組み honegumi framework; skeleton

覆う ōu to cover

PART 10

まだ mada still

郵便局 yūbin kyoku post office

役所 yakusho government office

案内する annai suru to guide; to inform

…が …ga but

存在する sonzai suru to exist

仮設の kasetsu no temporary

避難所 hinanjo shelter; evacuation center

町 machi town

立ち直る tachinaoru to recover; to rebuild

確実な kakujitsu na certain; sure

きざし kizashi sign; indication

はっきりと hakkiri to clearly; distinctly

PART 11

学校 gakkō school

体育館 taiikukan gymnasium

地元 jimoto local; hometown

破壊する hakai suru to destroy

跡形もなく atokata mo naku without a trace

消える kieru to disappear

(…て) しまう (... te) shimau to end up ...ing (with sense of regret) (following a verb in the **te**-form)

地区 chiku district; area

名前 namae name

書く kaku to write

掲げる kakageru to raise; to post

しっかりした shikkari shita solid; firm

海 umi sea

流される nagasareru to be swept away (passive form of 流す nagasu to sweep away)

はるかに haruka ni by far

強固な kyōko na strong; sturdy

形 katachi shape; form

PART 12

食料 shokuryō food

水 mizu water

風呂 furo bath

時間 jikan time

注意深く chūibukaku carefully; attentively

分けられる wakerareru to be divided (passive form of 分ける wakeru to divide)

無駄がないように muda ga nai yō ni so that nothing is wasted

分配 bunpai distribution

主婦 shufu housewife

教師 kyōshi teacher

消防士 shōbōshi firefighter

年長 nenchō older (children)

子供 kodomo children

余震 yoshin aftershock

年少 nenshō younger (children)

教える oshieru to teach; to instruct

喧嘩する kenka suru to fight

PART 13

外 soto outside

温泉リゾート onsen rizōto hot springs resort

追加の tsuika no additional

仮設 kasetsu temporary

改装 kaisō renovation; conversion

高齢者 **kōrei-sha** elderly person

住まわせる **sumawaseru** to house; to let (someone) live (modified causative form of 住む **sumu** to live)

PART 14

毎日 **mainichi** every day

何百人も **nanbyaku-nin mo** hundreds of people

運ばれる **hakobareru** to be transported (passive form of 運ぶ **hakobu** to transport)

心理的に **shinriteki ni** psychologically

助け **tasuke** help; support

二週間に一度 **nishūkan ni ichido** once every two weeks

PART 15

大切な **taisetsu na** important; precious

我慢する **gaman suru** to endure; to be patient

大変な **taihen na** difficult; hard

理解する **rikai suru** to understand

ルールを破る **rūru o yaburu** to break the rules

噂 **uwasa** rumor

広まる **hiromaru** to spread

崩壊する **hōkai suru** to collapse

PART 16

一緒に **issho ni** together

再建 **saiken** reconstruction

棺 **hitsugi** coffin

覆われる **ōwareru** to be covered (passive form of 覆う **ōu** to cover)

ヨウ素 **yōso** iodine

セシウム **seshiumu** cesium

プルトニウム **purutoniumu** plutonium

流出 **ryūshutsu** leakage; outflow

止まる **tomaru** to stop

心に残る **kokoro ni nokoru** to remain in the heart; to leave a lasting impression

なによりも **nani-yori mo** above all

危機 **kiki** crisis

立ち振る舞う **tachi-furumau** to behave; to conduct oneself

PART 17

笑顔 **egao** smile

手 **te** hand

押し込む **oshikomu** to push in

老人 **rōjin** elderly person

Shinsai go ni nihon ga sara ni suki ni natta riyū

思い出す omoidasu to remember; to recall

PART 18

素晴らしい subarashii wonderful; splendid

気質 kishitsu temperament; character

遺伝子 idenshi gene

長い年月をかけて nagai nengetsu o kakete over a long period of time

育まれる hagukumareru to be nurtured; to be fostered (passive form of 育む hagukumu to nurture)

社会的な shakaiteki na social

生活 seikatsu life; lifestyle

厳しい kibishii harsh; strict

顕著に kencho ni remarkably; noticeably

理由が何であれ riyū ga nan de are whatever the reason may be

確かに tashika ni certainly; surely

意味を持つ imi o motsu to have meaning

Comprehension and Language

Select the most appropriate answer in the parentheses or fill in the gap.

1. 2011年3月11日、東北で地震と津波が起き、一週間後、（福島・岩手）第一原発がメルトダウンし、漏れた放射能が危険だという報道が流れた。

2. 周囲の状況が厳しい中、たくさんの日本人は平然と日常生活を送っているようだった。これは敬服すべき＿＿＿＿だと思われた。

3. 陸前高田は泥水（が・で）町を根こそぎにされた。

4. 避難所では食料、水、風呂の時間は注意深く分けられ、＿＿＿＿がないように分配されていた。

5. 主婦、教師、＿＿＿＿＿がリーダーシップを取った。
6. 年長の子供たちは余震のときに何をすべきかを＿＿＿＿＿の子供たちに教えていた。
7. 誰が何をもらったかどうかなどと言って喧嘩することは（よくあった・なかった）。
8. 温泉リゾートでは皆がお風呂に＿＿＿週間に一度だけ入れた。
9. 誰一人として、リゾートのスタッフでさえ、このルールを＿＿＿＿＿人はいなかった。

Discussion Points

1. How did traditional Japanese values, such as perseverance (*gaman*) and community cooperation, influence the way people responded to the Tohoku earthquake and tsunami of 2011?

2. Do you think your community is ready to respond effectively to a large-scale natural disaster, such as an earthquake or hurricane? What steps could be taken to improve preparedness? How do cultural values or community structures influence disaster response in your area?

Dealing with Godless Japan
by Boye Lafayette De Mente

Author Boye Lafayette De Mente compares Western Christian morality with the philosophical and spiritual forces that are prevalent in Japan.

Key words

神 **kami** god

集団 **shūdan** group; organization

道徳 **dōtoku** morality; ethics

Part 1

The core of the difference between Western morality and Japanese morality is bound up in the religious systems that came to dominate the two cultures. In the West, Christianity became the dominant philosophical and spiritual force. It was based on absolute principles of good and bad, right and wrong.

Part 2

Christianity became a detailed code of thought and behavior that was drummed into Westerners from childhood. Every thought and action

無神論の日本と向き合う
Mushinron no nihon to mukiau
ボイ・ラファイエット・デ・メンテ

Part 1

西洋の道徳と日本の道徳との根本的な違いは、それぞれの文化に大きな影響を与えた宗教体系が違うことに由来する。西洋では、キリスト教が哲学的・精神的な面で大きな影響力を持ち、それは善悪や正誤といった絶対的な原則を通して影響力を発揮した。

Part 2

キリスト教は、西洋人の物事の考え方や行動の細かい指針となり、それは幼いときから徹底的に教え込まれた。彼らの考え方や行動は、唯一の全能、全知の神によって定められ、判断されて

was prescribed and judged by a single, all-powerful, all-knowing God. All the precepts pertaining to life were expressed in absolute terms.

Part 3

Westerners were conditioned to pass judgment on every aspect of life, labeling every thought, every action, as good or bad, moral or immoral. Life in the West was ruled by absolute principles, starting with the Ten Commandments. People were conditioned to suffer emotional and spiritual pain if they broke any of the Commandments, even when their "misbehavior" was unknown to others. God knew, and would take his revenge.

Part 4

For several hundred years in premodern Europe, the Roman Catholic Church carried on a vendetta against unbelievers and suspected unbelievers—a period of rampant religious intolerance and cruelty known as the Inquisition. Hundreds of thousands of people were imprisoned by the Church, tortured unmercifully and killed—frequently by burning.

Part 5

While the methods of Christianity were both inhuman and irrational, they nevertheless instilled in Westerners the precepts of behavior based on absolute, immutable principles. The prime directive of Western culture was that everyone should be conditioned to automatically distinguish between right and wrong as prescribed by the Church.

きた。人生に関わるすべての教えは、明確で揺るぎない絶対的な言葉で表現されていた。

Part 3
　西洋人は、人生のあらゆる面において判断を下すように教え込まれ、すべての考え方や行動を善悪、道徳的か非道徳的かと区別してきた。西洋での生き方は、十戒に始まる絶対的な原則によって支配されていた。人々は、たとえ自分の「不品行」が他人に知られなくても、戒律を破ると精神的・感情的な苦痛を感じるように教え込まれていた。神はすべてを知っており、「不品行」には罰が与えられるというようにだ。

Part 4
　近世以前のヨーロッパで、数百年にわたり、ローマ・カトリック教会が異教徒や異教徒と疑われた者に対して報復を行った。この時代は、異端審問（インクイジション）という宗教的な不寛容と残虐行為が横行した時代であった。何十万人もの人々が教会によって投獄され、無慈悲に拷問され、殺された。火あぶりにされることもよくあった。

Part 5
　過去にはキリスト教の方法は非人道的で非合理的だった時代もあったが、それでも西洋人に絶対的で不変の原則に基づく行動規範を教え込んだのだった。西洋文化の最も重要な指針は、すべての人が教会の定めた善悪の区別を自動的に行えるようにすることだった。

Part 6

In Japan, on the other hand, there was no single, omnipotent God. There were no Ten Commandments. There were no religious texts that taught absolute truths. There were detailed guidelines for behavior, but they were matters of social status, position, gender, relationships and the like; they had nothing to do with religious tenets.

Part 7

Among the Japanese, ultimate power was not in the hands of a god. It was in the hands of their group. They swore allegiance and oaths to the members of their groups and to their group leaders. They did not make vows to a god. Nor did they fear or promise obedience to their gods; they feared the opinions and judgments of the individual members of their immediate groups, and they did their best to conform to the majority opinion and to the wishes of their superiors.

Part 8

In this cultural context, when the setting and circumstances were peaceful, what was true and what was moral was determined by the majority. In times of conflict and chaos, when the center of power changed, truth and morality also changed to conform to the new circumstances. In other words, the virtuous Japanese were those who stayed in harmony with their fellow group members by obeying all of the rules of etiquette demanded by their social system, precisely followed the consensus of the group, and protected the group from all outsiders. There was no absolute good. There was only the immediate needs of the many. Whatever

Part 6

一方、日本には唯一の全能の神はいなかった。十戒もなかった。絶対的な真理を教える宗教的な文書も存在しなかった。行動の指針は細かく定められていたが、それらは社会的な地位、立場、性別、人間関係などに関するもので、宗教的な教えとは関係がなかった。

Part 7

日本人にとって、究極の権力は神の手にはなく、彼らの属する集団の手にあった。日本人は自分の属する集団の仲間や指導者に忠誠を誓い、単一の神に誓いを立てることはなかった。また、神々を恐れたり、神々に服従を誓ったりすることもなかった。彼らが恐れたのは、自分の直属の集団の個々のメンバーの意見や判断であり、多数派の意見や上司の希望に合わせるよう努めていた。

Part 8

この文化的背景の中で、平和な状況では、何が真実で何が道徳的かは多数派によって決定された。一方、紛争や混乱のときに権力の中心が変わると、真実や道徳も新たな状況に合わせて変わった。つまり、徳のある日本人とは、社会制度が求めるすべての規律や礼儀作法を守り、自分の集団の合意したことにきちんと従い、外部の脅威から集団を守り、集団内の仲間との調和を保つ者たちだった。絶対的な善は存在しなかった。ただ多数派の目先のニーズが存在するだけだった。多数派にとって都合の

served the needs of the majority was good; whatever didn't was bad. By extension of this situational morality, whatever benefited group leaders in Japanese society was also good for group members. (Of course, this mentality is one of the reasons why Japanese leaders have traditionally been able to engage in all kinds of economic, financial and political skulduggery without incurring the wrath of their underlings.)

Part 9

The first Westerners in Japan, conditioned in absolute principles that, right or wrong, covered virtually every aspect of human thought and behavior, were shocked when they encountered the circumstantial and human-centered morality of the Japanese.

Part 10

Today, as a result of the introduction of democratic principles into Japan by the United States following the end of World War II in 1945, and subsequent decades of Western influence, the moral system that grew out of Japan's unique blend of Buddhism, Confucianism, Taoism and Shinto has been watered down considerably, but it is still very much in evidence, particularly in the government and in traditional organizations, including many corporations.

良いものが善であり、都合の悪いものが悪だった。この状況的な道徳観の延長線上で、集団の指導者にとって利益となることは、その集団の仲間にとっても良いこととされた。(もちろん、この思考様式が、日本の指導者たちが伝統的にいろいろな経済的、金融的、政治的な悪を行いながらも、部下の怒りを買わずに済んできた理由の一つだ。)

Part 9
　最初に日本を訪れた西洋人たちは、自分たちは考え方や行動の絶対的な原則を教え込まれてきていたため、日本人の状況に応じた人間中心の道徳観に驚かされた。

Part 10
　1945年の第二次世界大戦終結後は、アメリカによって日本に民主主義の原則が導入され、その後、数十年、西洋の影響を受けた。その結果、日本の仏教、儒教、道教、神道の独自の融合から生まれた日本独自の道徳体系はかなり薄れてきたが、依然として見られる部分も多く、特に政府や伝統的な組織、そして多くの企業ではそれが顕著だ。

Vocabulary and Expressions

PART 1

西洋の **seiyō no** Western

道徳 **dōtoku** morality; ethics

根本的な **konponteki na** fundamental; basic

違い **chigai** difference

それぞれの **sorezore no** each; respective

文化 **bunka** culture

影響 **eikyō** influence; impact

与える **ataeru** to give

宗教 **shūkyō** religion

体系 **taikei** system; structure

由来 **yurai** origin

キリスト教 **Kirisuto-kyō** Christianity

哲学 **tetsugaku** philosophy

…的な **...teki na** suffix used to turn a noun into an adjective

精神 **seishin** spirit; mind

面 **men** aspect

…力 **...ryoku** power of ...

持つ **motsu** to have; to possess

善 **zen** good

悪 **aku** evil

善悪 **zen'aku** good and evil

正誤 **seigo** right and wrong

絶対的な **zettaiteki na** absolute

原則 **gensoku** principle

…を通して **... o tōshite** through ...; via ...

発揮する **hakki suru** to demonstrate; to exert

PART 2

西洋人 **seiyōjin** Westerner; Western people

物事 **monogoto** things; matters

考え方 **kangaekata** way of thinking

行動 **kōdō** action; behavior

細かい **komakai** detailed

指針 **shishin** guideline; direction

幼い **osanai** very young

徹底的に **tetteiteki ni** thoroughly; completely

教え込まれる **oshiekomareru** to be taught deeply (passive form of 教え込む **oshiekomu** to teach deeply)

唯一の **yuiitsu no** the only; sole

全能の zennō no omnipotent

全知の zenchi no omniscient

神 kami god

…によって … ni yotte by …; according to …

定められる sadamerareru to be determined (passive form of 定める sadameru to determine)

判断 handan judgment; decision

(…て)くる …te kuru to come to …; to have … (following a verb in the te-form)

人生 jinsei life

…に関わる … ni kakawaru related to …

すべての subete no all; every

教え oshie teaching; doctrine

明確な meikaku na clear; distinct

揺るぎない yuruginai unshakable; unwavering

言葉 kotoba word; language

表現 hyōgen expression; representation

PART 3

あらゆる arayuru all; every

下す kudasu to hand down; to issue (a decision)

道徳的 dōtokuteki moral

非道徳的 hidōtokuteki immoral

区別する kubetsu suru to distinguish; to differentiate

生き方 ikikata way of life

十戒 jikkai the Ten Commandments

…に始まる … ni hajimaru starting from …; beginning with …

原則 gensoku principle; rule

支配 shihai control; domination

たとえ(…ない) tatoe (…nai) even if (isn't/aren't …)

自分 jibun oneself; self

不品行 fuhinkō misconduct; misbehavior

他人 tannin other people; others

知られる shirareru to be known; to become known (passive form of 知る shiru to get to know)

戒律 kairitsu commandment; precept

破る yaburu to break; to violate

精神的な seishinteki na spiritual

感情的な kanjōteki na emotional

苦痛 kutsū pain; suffering

感じる kanjiru to feel; to sense

…ように **...yō ni** in such a way ...; so that ... (following a verb in the plain non-past form)

罰 **batsu** punishment

与えられる **ataeraru** to be given (passive form of 与える **ataeru** to give)

PART 4

近世以前の **kinsei-izen no** premodern

数百年にわたり **sūhyaku-nen ni watari** over the course of several hundred years

教会 **kyōkai** church

異教徒 **ikyōto** heretic; unbeliever

疑われる **utagawareru** to be suspected (passive form of 疑う **utagau** to suspect)

者 **mono** person; individual

…に対して **... ni taishite** against ...; toward ...

報復 **hōfuku** retaliation; revenge

行う **okonau** to carry out; to perform

時代 **jidai** era; period

異端審問 **itan shinmon** the Inquisition

…という **...to iu** called ...; known as ...

不寛容 **fukanyō** intolerance

残虐行為 **zangyaku kōi** cruelty; brutal act

横行する **ōkō suru** to be rampant; to prevail

何十万人もの人々 **nanjūman-nin mo no hitobito** hundreds of thousands of people

投獄 **tōgoku** imprisonment

無慈悲に **mujihi ni** mercilessly; ruthlessly

拷問 **gōmon** torture

殺される **korosareru** to be killed (passive form of 殺す **korosu** to kill)

火あぶり **hi-aburi** burning at the stake

PART 5

過去 **kako** the past

方法 **hōhō** method; way

非人道的 **hijindōteki** inhumane

非合理的 **higōriteki** irrational

不変の… **fuhen no ...** unchanging ...; immutable ...

原則 **gensoku** principle

…に基づく **... ni motozuku** based on ...

規範 **kihan** standard; norm

最も mottomo most

重要 jūyō important

自動的 jidōteki automatic

…ようにする …yō ni suru to make it so … (following a verb in the plain non-past form)

PART 6

一方 ippō on the other hand

真理 shinri truth

文書 bunsho document; text

存在する sonzai suru to exist

細かい komakai detailed

社会 shakai society

地位 chii status; position

立場 tachiba position; standpoint

性別 seibetsu gender

人間 ningen human; person

関係 kankei relationship

…に関する … ni kansuru related to …

教え oshie teaching; doctrine

PART 7

…にとって … ni totte for …; in terms of …

究極の kyūkyoku no ultimate

権力 kenryoku power; authority

手 te hand

属する zokusuru to belong to

集団 shūdan group; organization

仲間 nakama comrades; members of a group

指導者 shidō-sha leader

忠誠 chūsei loyalty

誓う chikau to vow; to swear

単一の… tan'itsu no … single …; one …

神 kami god

誓いを立てる chikai o tateru to make a vow

神々 kamigami gods

恐れる osoreru to fear

(…た)り (… ta)ri to do …; etc. (following a verb in the ta-form)

服従 fukujū obedience; submission

直属の chokusoku no immediately belonging to

個々の… koko no … individual …

意見 iken opinion

多数派 tasūha majority

上司 jōshi superior; boss

Mushinron no nihon to mukiau

希望 kibō hope; desire

合わせる awaseru to match; to align

努める tsutomeru to strive; to endeavor

PART 8

背景 haikei background

平和な heiwa na peaceful

状況 jōkyō situation; condition

真実 shinjitsu truth; reality

決定 kettei decision

紛争 fun'sō conflict; dispute

混乱 konran chaos; confusion

中心 chūshin center; core

変わる kawaru to change

新たな arata na new

徳のある toku no aru virtuous; moral

制度 seido system

求める motomeru to seek; to demand

規律 kiritsu discipline

礼儀作法 reigi sahō etiquette; manners

守る mamoru to protect; to observe

合意 gōi consensus; agreement

きちんと kichinto properly; neatly

従う shitagau to obey; to follow

外部 gaibu external; outside

脅威 kyōi threat

…内 ...nai inside ...; within ...

調和 chōwa harmony

保つ tamotsu to maintain; to keep

目先の mesaki no immediate; short-term

都合の良い tsugō no yoi convenient; favorable

都合が悪い tsugō ga warui inconvenient; unfavorable

道徳観 dōtokukan moral view; sense of morality

延長線上で enchōsenjō de in the extension of; along the lines of

利益 rieki benefit; profit

思考様式 shikō yōshiki way of thinking; mindset

伝統的に dentōteki ni traditionally

いろいろな iroiro na various

経済的 keizaiteki economic

金融的 kin'yūteki financial

政治的 seijiteki political

…ながらも ...nagara mo although ...

部下 buka subordinate

怒りを買わずに済む ikari o kawazu ni sumu to avoid incurring anger

理由 riyū reason

PART 9

最初に saisho ni at first; initially

訪れる otozureru to visit

…に応じた ... ni ōjita in response to ...

人間 ningen human being

驚かされる odorokasareru to be surprised (passive form of 驚かす odorokasu to surprise)

PART 10

1945年 1945-nen 1945

第二次世界大戦 dai-niji sekai taisen World War II

終結 shūketsu end; conclusion

…後 ...go after ...

民主主義 minshu-shugi democracy

導入 dōnyū introduction

数十年 sūjū-nen several decades

受ける ukeru to receive

その結果 sono kekka as a result of that

仏教 Bukkyō Buddhism

儒教 Jukyō Confucianism

道教 Dōkyō Taoism

神道 Shintō Shinto

独自の dokuji no unique; original

融合 yūgō fusion; blending

生まれる umareru to be born

かなり kanari considerably; quite

薄れる usureru to fade; to weaken

それでも soredemo nevertheless; even so

依然として izen toshite still; as before

部分 bubun part; portion

多い ōi many; much

特に toku ni especially; particularly

政府 seifu government

組織 soshiki organization

企業 kigyō company

顕著な kencho na prominent; remarkable

Comprehension and Language

Select the most appropriate answer in the parentheses or fill in the gap.

1. 西洋の道徳と日本の道徳との根本的な違いは、それぞれの文化に大きな影響を与えた＿＿＿＿体系が違うことに由来する。
2. キリスト教は、西洋人の物事の考え方や行動の（大まかな・細かい）指針となった。
3. すべての考え方や行動を善か悪か、道徳的か＿＿＿＿道徳的かと区別してきた。
4. 西洋人は戒律を破ると＿＿＿＿を受けると思っていた。
5. 日本には唯一の全能の神は（いた・いなかった）。
6. 日本人は自分の属する＿＿＿＿の仲間や指導者に忠誠を誓っていた。
7. 西洋人たちは考え方や行動の絶対的な原則に基づいた道徳観を持っていたが、日本人は（状況・戒律）に応じた人間中心の道徳観を持っていた。

Discussion Points

1. What are the advantages of society-based morality that most Japanese people tend to practice, as described in this essay?
2. What are the advantages of God-based Western morality that followers of religions like Christianity tend to practice, as described in this essay?
3. If you observe your boss committing a wrongdoing, would you try to correct them?

Appendix I: Verb Forms

	Plain affirmative non-past form or dictionary form	Plain negative non-past form or nai-form	Plain affirmative past form or ta-form	Plain negative past form or nakatta-form	Stem form	te-form
Class I regular verbs (ru- or ichidan verbs)	たべる	たべない	たべた	たべなかった	たべ	たべて
	みる	みない	みた	みなかった	み	みて
Class II regular verbs (u- or godan verbs)	とる	とらない	とった	とらなかった	とり	とって
	かく	かかない	かいた	かかなかった	かき	かいて
	およぐ	およがない	およいだ	およがなかった	およぎ	およいで
	おす	おさない	おした	おさなかった	おし	おして
	かう	かわない	かった	かわなかった	かい	かって
	かつ	かたない	かった	かたなかった	かち	かって
	のむ	のまない	のんだ	のまなかった	のみ	のんで
	しぬ	しなない	しんだ	しななかった	しに	しんで
	とぶ	とばない	とんだ	とばなかった	とび	とんで
Irregular verbs	する	しない	した	しなかった	し	して
	くる	こない	きた	こなかった	き	きて

Volitional form	Potential form	Passive form	Causative form	ba-conditional form	Negative ba-conditional form	Command form
たべよう	たべ(ら)れる	たべられる	たべさせる	たべれば	たべなければ	たべろ
みよう	み(ら)れる	みられる	みさせる	みれば	みなければ	みろ
とろう	とれる	とられる	とらせる	とれば	とらなければ	とれ
かこう	かける	かかれる	かかせる	かけば	かかなければ	かけ
およごう	およげる	およがれる	およがせる	およげば	およがなければ	およげ
おそう	おせる	おされる	おさせる	おせば	おさなければ	おせ
かおう	かえる	かわれる	かわせる	かえば	かわなければ	かえ
かとう	かてる	かたれる	かたせる	かてば	かたなければ	かて
のもう	のめる	のまれる	のませる	のめば	のまなければ	のめ
しのう	しねる	しなれる	しなせる	しねば	しななければ	しね
とぼう	とべる	とばれる	とばせる	とべば	とばなければ	とべ
しよう	できる	される	させる	すれば	しなければ	しろ
こよう	こ(ら)れる	こられる	こさせる	くれば	こなければ	こい

Appendix II: Adjective Forms

	Plain affirmative non-past form	Plain negative non-past form	Plain affirmative past form	Plain negative past form
i-adjective	ながい	ながくない	ながかった	ながくなかった
na-adjective	ひまだ	ひまじゃない	ひまだった	ひまじゃなかった

	Stem form	te-form	Pre-nominal form	ba-conditional form
i-adjective	なが	ながくて	ながい	ながければ
na-adjective	ひま	ひまで	ひまな	ひまであれば

Answer Key

Sexual Minority Rights: 1. かり(借り) 2. ふか(不可) 3. こんなん(困難) 4. めいじ(明治) 5. に 6. パートナーシップ 7. いけん(違憲) 8. そうぞく(相続) 9. うけいれる(受け入れる) 10. こと

Cosplay: 1. コスチューム 2. しゅみ(趣味) 3. レイヤー 4. カメコ 5. で 6. つくられ(作られ) 7. コミケ 8. 広がった

Nature and the Environment: 1. に 2. リサイクル 3. かわかして(乾かして) 4. さくげん(削減) 5. プラスチック 6. あり 7. こくふく(克服)

The Origins of Sake: 1. しんわ(神話) 2. ふるい(古い) 3. よう 4. 794 5. おこなわれて(行われて) 6. と 7. にも 8. みず(水)

Maiko: 1. いえる(言える) 2. みならい(見習い) 3. おきや(置屋) 4. こと 5. いなくなって 6. きそく(規則)

Omae: 1. さけ(避け) 2. えらぶ(選ぶ) 3. いじめ 4. する 5. おまえ(お前) 6. だった 7. と 8. せきにん(責任) 9. たちば(立場)

Aging Japan: 1. まで 2. あった(合った) 3. か(化) 4. りつ(率) 5. あきや(空き家) 6. ろうどう(労働) 7. べき 8. しなければ

Is K-Pop Beating J-Pop?: 1. で 2. にほんじん(日本人) 3. だんせい(男性) 4. SMAP 5. SNS 6. たり 7. ビジュアル 8. かも

Irezumi: 1. かくれる(隠れる) 2. かくす(隠す) 3. せいよう(西洋) 4. みせ(見せ) 5. ぼうりょくだん(暴力団) 6. されて 7. はらう(払う)

Japanese Women: 1. ひくい(低い) 2. えらばれた(選ばれた) 3. カイロ 4. ちじ(知事) 5. なくて 6. ヨーロッパ 7. だいひょうとりしまりやく(代表取締役) 8. 138 9. おわった(終わった) 10. ふやす(増やす)

Why Are the Japanese So Bad at English?: 1. アジア 2. にている(似ている) 3. せい 4. られて 5. で 6. しれない 7. べきではない 8. はじめた 9. おそ(遅)

Suicide Rate: 1. たかい(高い) 2. な 3. と 4. はじ(恥) 5. が 6. しまう 7. セラピスト 8. へんけん(偏見) 9. ず 10. ない

Japan's Way of Working: 1. じょれつ(序列) 2. ほうかい(崩壊) 3. がいしけい(外資系) 4. せいべつ(性別) 5. いけん(意見) 6. じんじ(人事) 7. とって

Japan's Drinking Culture: 1. ない 2. ばんざい(万歳) 3. めいじ(明治) 4. あげる 5. もらう 6. で 7. ような 8. じょうし(上司) 9. しじ(支持)

Dating: 1. に 2. を 3. する 4. ごうコン(合コン) 5. あつまる(集まる) 6. ばしょ(場所) 7. に

Why I Love Japan: 1. ふくしま(福島) 2. のうりょく(能力) 3. で 4. むだ(無駄) 5. しょうぼうし(消防士) 6. ねんしょう(年少) 7. なかった 8. に(二) 9. やぶる(破る)

Godless Japan: 1. しゅうきょう(宗教) 2. こまかい(細かい) 3. ひ(非) 4. ばつ(罰) 5. いなかった 6. しゅうだん(集団) 7. じょうきょう(状況)

References

Sexual Minority Rights

Elaine Lies, "In landmark ruling, Japan court says not allowing same-sex marriage is 'unconstitutional'," Reuters, Mar 17, 2021. www.todayonline.com/world/landmark-ruling-japan-court-says-not-allowing-same-sex-marriage-unconstitutional

Shaimaa Khalil, "Marriage equality eludes Japan's same-sex couples," BBC, Oct 2, 2023. www.bbc.com/news/world-asia-66173433

Gary Leupp, *Male Colors: The Construction of Homosexuality in Tokugawa Japan*, University of California Press, 1995.

Cosplay: The Art of Dressing Up

Héctor García, *A Geek in Japan*, Tuttle, 2019

Nature and the Environment

Devayani Khare and Pui Yi Wong, "Japan's plastic waste exports—and how to slow them down," Break Free From Plastic, Sep 23, 2022. www.breakfreefromplastic.org/2022/09/23/japan's-plastic-waste-exports-and-how-to-slow-them-down/

"First Generation Prius Hybrid Petrol-Electric Car," Science Museum Group. collection.sciencemuseumgroup.org.uk/objects/co8566796/first-generation-prius-hybrid-petrol-electric-car

Naoko Tochibayashi and Naoko Kutty, "Hydrogen is developing fast in Japan, closer to societal use," The World Economic Forum, Apr 10, 2024. www.weforum.org/stories/2024/04/hydrogen-japan

The Origins of Sake

Nancy Matsumoto and Michael Tremblay, *Exploring the World of Japanese Craft Sake: Rice, Water, Earth*, Tuttle, 2022

Maiko, Apprentice Geisha

Alix Tunell, "Confessions of a Maiko, Japan's Geisha-in-Training," Mar 29, 2018, Refinery 29. www.refinery29.com/en-us/japanese-maiko-beauty-routine

"An Insight into Japan's Modern Geisha," Journeyman Pictures, 2003. www.youtube.com/watch?v=YSrhCEHyB0U

Kumiko Nishio, "Geiko, Maiko, Ochaya, and Okiya," 2010, Taylor & Francis Online. doi.org/10.2753/JES1097-203X370402

Omae: A Question of Language

"*Ijime izoku ni 'omae' kyōiku-chō jii, Niigata, Shibata*" (Addressing bullying victim's bereaved family as "omae": Superintendent of education expresses his intent to resign), *Nikkei Keizai Shimbun*, Oct 11, 2018. www.nikkei.com/article/DGXMZO36375630R11C18A0CC1000/

"*Ijime jisatsu seito no chichi ni 'omae' shikyōiku-chō ga jinin Niigata*" (Niigata Superintendent of Education resigns after calling father of student who committed suicide 'omae'), *The Sankei Shimbun*, Oct 11, 2018. www.sankei.com/article/20181011-3HYNUPP6TZNKPO7IXQXLH3TGD4/

"*Ijime jisatsu no oya o 'omae' to yobi Shibata-shi kyōiku-chō ga jinin*" (Shibata City Superintendent of Education resigns after calling parent of bullied suicide victim 'omae'), FC2, Oct 11, 2018. rann0319.blog.fc2.com/blog-entry-352.html

Aging Japan

Chris Burgess, "Japan's multiculturalism fails to keep pace with rising migration," East Asia Forum, Jun 5, 2024. eastasiaforum.org/2024/06/05/japans-multiculturalism-fails-to-keep-pace-with-rising-migration/

Chris Lau and Mayumi Maruyama, "Super-aged Japan now has 9 million vacant homes. And that's a problem," CNN World, May 7, 2024. edition.cnn.com/2024/05/07/asia/akiya-homes-problem-japan-intl-hnk/index.html

"*Gin-san no wakasa no himitsu*" (Gin-san's secret to staying young), Min-Iren, Apr 1, 2004. www.min-iren.gr.jp/news-press/genki/20040401_3037.html

Mari Yamaguchi, "Japan had the fewest babies it has ever recorded last year," AP, Feb 27, 2024. apnews.com/article/japan-births-aging-population-7b0639bda2f2f8982fbb19789eb1f1a0#

"*Sekai sai kōrei wa Ashiya-shi zaijū no 116-sai no josei*" (World's oldest person is a 116-year-old woman living in Ashiya), NHK News Web, Aug 21, 2024. www3.nhk.or.jp/lnews/kobe/20240821/2020026116.html

World Social Report 2023, "Leaving No One Behind In An Aging World," United Nations. www.un.org/development/desa/dspd/wp-content/uploads/sites/22/2023/01/2023wsr-fullreport.pdf

"World's oldest twin dies at 107," BBC News, Jan 23, 2000. news.bbc.co.uk/2/hi/asia-pacific/615413.stm

Is K-Pop Beating J-Pop in the Globalization of Asian Music?

Charlie Harding and Nate Sloan, "How Megan Thee Stallion brought Japanese hip hop to the Hot 100," podcast Switched on Pop Vulture, Sep 17, 2024. switchedonpop.com

Elaine Kathryn Andres, "1963. Sukiyaki by Kyu Sakamoto," American Experience Newsletter, Jun 9, 2017. www.pbs.org/wgbh/americanexperience/features/songs-of-the-summer-1963/

Jayson M Chun, "Languages of the Pop Pacific (part 1)—Korean," International Institute for Asian Studies, Dec 14, 2023. blog.iias.asia/pop-pacific/languages-pop-pacific-part-1-korean

Jayson M Chun, "What is J-pop and K-pop? (part 2)—K-pop innovations REMIX," International Institute for Asian Studies, May 13, 2024. blog.iias.asia/pop-pacific/what-j-pop-and-k-pop-part-2-k-pop-innovations-remix

Naomi Gingold, "Why The Blueprint For K-Pop Actually Came From Japan," NPR, Jan 8, 2019. www.npr.org/2019/01/08/683339743/why-the-blueprint-for-k-pop-actually-came-from-japan

Irezumi: Japan's Underground Tattoo Culture

Brian Ashcraft and Hori Benny, *Japanese Tattoos: History, Culture*, Tuttle, 2016.

Japanese Women Break the Iron Ceiling

"Asia Game Changer Awards—Yuriko Koike," Asia Society, 2019. asiasociety.org/asia-game-changer-awards/yuriko-koike

"Global Gender Gap Report 2023," World Economic Forum. www3.weforum.org/docs/WEF_GGGR_2023.pdf

Miho Uranaka and Rocky Swift, "Suntory Beverage's first female CEO wants more women managers, global business," Reuters, Dec 20, 2022. www.reuters.com/business/retail-consumer/suntory-beverages-first-female-ceo-wants-more-women-managers-global-business

"*Nichigin ni hatsu no josei riji, Shimizu Nagoya shitencho ga shunin,*" (Shimizu, general manager of the Nagoya branch, appointed first female director of BOJ) *Nihon Keizai Shimbun*, May 11, 2020. www.nikkei.com/article/DGXMZO58928200R10C20A5EAF000/

Tania Chen and Toru Fujioka, "BOJ's former top female executive takes gender fight to Japan's schools," *The Japan Times*, Jul 27, 2004. www.japantimes.co.jp/business/2024/07/27/tokiko-shimizu-boj-gender-schools

"The World's Most Powerful Women," Forbes, 2023. www.forbesafrica.com/lists/2023/12/06/the-worlds-most-powerful-women/

Why Are the Japanese So Bad at English?

"English Proficiency Index," Education First, 2023. www.ef.com

Jack Tarrant, "Tokyo great-grandmother proves it's never too late to learn," Reuters, Mar 11, 2019. www.reuters.com/article/sports/tokyo-great-grandmother-proves-it-s-never-too-late-to-learn-idUSL5N20S0M1/

Japan's High Suicide Rate

"*Tōdai-sotsu erīto bijo ga jisatsu made ni tsudzutta ʾkumon no sakebi' 50-tsū*," (50 "cries of agony" written by Tokyo University graduate elite pretty woman before suicide) *The Sankei Shimbun*, Oct 22, 2016. www.sankei.com/article/20161022-NVADFKTPLNJ7ZOBUNNGTLIYMOA/

"Preventing Suicide: A Global Imperative," World Health Organization, 2014.

"Number of Suicides in Japan Rises in 2022," Nippon.com, Mar 27, 2023. www.nippon.com/en/japan-data/h01624/

"Suicide Rates," OECD, accessed Oct 2024. www.oecd.org/en/data/indicators/suicide-rates.html

Taraneh Mojaverian, Takeshi Hashimoto, and Heejung S. Kim, "Cultural differences in professional help seeking: A comparison of Japan and the US," *Frontiers in Psychology 3*, Jan 11, 2013. www.frontiersin.org/journals/psychology/articles/10.3389/fpsyg.2012.00615/full

Ryann Tanap, "Why Asian-Americans and Pacific Islanders Don't Go to Therapy," National Alliance on Mental Illness blog post, Jul 25, 2019. www.nami.org/asian-american-pacific-islander/why-asian-americans-and-pacific-islanders-dont-go-to-therapy/

Maxine Cheyney, "Changing the perception of mental health in Japan," Japan Today, Jun 9, 2018. japantoday.com/category/features/lifestyle/mindful-care-changing-the-perception-of-mental-health-in-japan

Transforming Japan's Way of Working

Toshiaki Komatsu, "*Sekai-teki ni mo mezurashī ʾshūshin koyō nenkōjoretsu' o tsudzukeru Nihon*," (Japan still has unique system of lifetime employment and seniority-based promotion), AllAbout, Feb 28, 2023. allabout.co.jp/gm/gc/496727/#google_vignette

Michelle Toh and Emiko Jozuka, "Japan's workers haven't had a raise in 30 years," CNN, Feb 3, 2023. edition.cnn.com/2023/02/03/business/japan-workers-wages-inflation-intl-hnk/index.html

"Japanese companies navigate workplace revolution as job hunters get choosier," *Nikkei Asia*, Apr 24, 2024. asia.nikkei.com/Spotlight/The-Big-Story/Japanese-companies-navigate-workplace-revolution-as-job-hunters-get-choosier

Japan's Drinking Culture

Chris Bunting, *Drinking Japan: A Guide to Japan's Best Drinks and Drinking Establishments*, Tuttle, 2011

Dating Opportunities

"Gokon," Japan Experience, Sep 27, 2018. www.japan-experience.com/plan-your-trip/to-know/understanding-japan/gokon

"*Isei ni ue sugi terukara jinsei-hatsu no machi kon ittemita kekka,*" (I'm so desperate for the opposite sex I went to my first ever machikon event), Yokkichanneru, YouTube. www.youtube.com/watch?v=u37BV2MWwqc

"*Gōkon kara kekkon shita*" (I got married through gokon), Rabbit Space, Nov 30, 2022. rabbitspace.net/column/5410/

Why I Love Japan Even More since the Earthquake

David McNeill, "Why I love Japan even more since the earthquake," *The Asia-Pacific Journal: Japan Focus*, Dec 31, 2012. apjjf.org/david-mcneill/4653/article

Dealing with Godless Japan

Boye Lafayette De Mente, *Japan Unmasked* Tuttle, 2006